The SEEDS of TOBY

The Continual Imperative of Holistic Criminal Justice Reform

DONAVAN BAILEY, LSW, EDD

First Edition

PAGE PUBLISHING
Conneaut Lake, PA

First originally published by Page Publishing 2024

ISBN 979-8-89553-312-3 (pbk)
ISBN 979-8-89553-334-5 (digital)

Printed in the United States of America

DEDICATION

This book is dedicated to The Baileynation. Esposita and four NextGen, thank you for putting up with me. As Mark Twain so famously wrote "The two most important days in your life are the day you are born and the day you find out why." I'm grateful for your existence and I hope in my feeble efforts that I help you enjoy the amazing privilege of life and find and fulfill your life purpose. Te Amo…

CONTENTS

ACKNOWLEDGEMENTS

Thank you to the original educator and critical thinker, Momma Bailey. Mom, I can remember as a kid when I called you at work, you would answer the phone in an educated voice and "The King's English" that I didn't recognize. It was very confusing then, but that ability to "codeswitch" and educationally adapt to whatever environment was a stamp on my educational identity. Also, thank you for the many debates you and the Uncle's had into the night, that had me waking up wondering what you were arguing about so late… heated discussions but critical thought in action. Also and as I allude to in this book, thank you for the family coffee table, Ebony Magazine flanking it, and always pointing out to myself and Big Bro's what it meant to be African, and American.

Also, thank you to the dearly departed Dr. Martin Luther King Jr. I used to watch and listen to your speeches like the modern-day online series binge-watch, and I was mesmerized by this image and voice of a genius African American man with scholarship, critical thought, depth, oration, and all coupled in a movement for the betterment of humanity; that breathed in me a discipline and identity of admiring and seeking scholarly thought/impact as a consistent part of my holistic diet.

Thank you to the former director of Rochester Network for Re-entry/Next Chapter Ministries. This blonde-haired, Euro-American man, rough and tough, farmer-type hands that showed he wasn't corporate, a former truck driver as I remember it, and so unassuming to be a leader in the criminal justice system. A man who started a residential program for those coming out of prison… I never said it, but I was often amazed at what you were called to do, the wisdom and care you had in doing it, and hilarious but awe-inspiring to me, the physical man this powerful purpose was embodied in. It was amazing daily, even more so amazing when the thoughts of this book began to ring in my head and flow to paper, you crazily listened and partnered with me in working out these many thoughts into community action, or shall we say valiant attempts. Thanks to your dear wife and family. Your legacy is powerful, lives on, and is seen in the programs you founded, led, as well as in the many people you impacted. Thanks for many impromptu conversations, debates, and disagreements around many criminal justice topics and certainly the topics in this book.

As thanks or acknowledgments go there are always too many to mention. But with respect to all those who impacted my identity and the feeble thoughts of this book, deep thanks. Above all, thank God…

INTRODUCTION

It was 1977. I was six years old, and I found myself mesmerized while I sat on the couch with my mother watching Roots, an old-school style TV miniseries. It was the binge-watch of its time but very different from the evolution of viewing your favorite series on 2020's various viewing formats, in that you had to wait for and cherish each episode week by week, with no streaming service or recording to catch up on all the episodes. In those days, as it was, television miniseries dramas were all the rage, and this television production, adapted from author Alex Haley's *Roots: The Saga of an American Family*, had specific significance as it portrayed the physical and cultural journey of Africans to African Americans in a vivid and frank display for its time. Of special note was the fact that this was a television phenomenon, one of the first of its kind, and still ranked as one of the best in TV history within popular culture. It had specific and special significance because it was a bold first of sorts that portrayed the enslavement of Africans and its extraordinary place in American history in an open and unabashed approach and just a decade away from the turbulent racial period in which America experienced various powerful events, such as the murder of civil rights leader, Dr. Martin Luther King Jr. in 1968, and the passage of the Civil Rights Act of 1964. This series was so impactful it became a hallmark of the African American community and television, positively branding such names as its author, Alex Haley, and actors Louis Gosset Jr., Cecily Tyson, Ben Vereen,

Leslie Uggums, Olivia Cole, and Lavar Burton. The original series spawned a tremendous contemporary remix, *Roots* 2016.

As I remember in the 1970s, sitting there as a child, I was a witness to this amazing and unprecedented cinematic feature. I remember a few things at that age, but I do remember my mother had me sitting there, watching this series with her in our Indianapolis home. It certainly could have been purposeful on her part to impact her youngest child, but I assume my mother just had me in the room with her just parenting, not thinking I was paying attention. The full frontal of this was unbelievable and mesmerizing. I was in awe with what I was seeing with a childish wonder, partly frightened but more so curious. What I didn't know about this was strangely futuristic, evolving identity, curiosity, and storing something to be unearthed later in my personal and professional journey.

As I learned later, there were many parts of this miniseries that were awe-inspiring and powerful. But on this day and to this child at the time, none was more jaw-dropping than one of the beginning sequences where slave Kunta Kinte, now forcefully relocated to America from his African home, was caught running from his new slave dwelling in hopes of getting back to his native land. As I remember it, he was caught and hung by his hands in the public square. Both slave and free were there to watch what was about to transpire. As he dangled, the slave owners proceeded to whip Kunta as it first seemed only as a consequence of absconding. However, more ardent while whipping the runaway slave, they asked him to say his American name, "Toby." As it was portrayed, this was a way of getting his merciless beating to stop and an attempt by Kunta's slave owners to make sure they internally and externally branded in Kunta his new land, new life, and new identity.

Bloody lash after bloody lash continued to cut into Kunta's back, with scream after scream. The slave owner gave Kunta an opportunity to cease the scourge if he were to speak his American name. But time after time, Kunta replied with his native name, "Kunta Kinte." As I watched as a kid in my childish dramatic style, this seemed to go on for days, Kunta would not say his American name. Forever would finally end as Kunta could not take the pain anymore, and in complete exhaustion, he gave in and said his American name, "Toby." At this moment, in theatrical fashion, this segment of the miniseries came to an end.

While this episode ended with fellow slaves pulling Toby from his hanging and tending to his horrifying beating, my memory and the consequent confusion of this episode did not. This was the first time I witnessed the magnitude of what little I knew, and the more I would come to know about the ugly curse and historic power of racism and slavery. On that day, I couldn't understand the why of what was displayed in this television series. As I grew older, that why became better understood, at least in the greater context of slavery and racism. But at that time, what I couldn't answer about that overwhelming scene of Kunta Kinta hanging and being brutally beaten was, "Why wouldn't he just say his American name, Toby, to get these evil men from stopping hitting him?" To my little mind, that seemed easy, at least to stop what was happening momentarily.

The answer to that question, as fulfilled and evolved in Haley's Roots saga, I believe, has extensive implications in what America has historically experienced and is experiencing in the American criminal justice system and many adjacent societal dynamics. Indeed, I believe what lies beneath the context of this scene is one of many next steps to what Michelle Alexander brilliantly called *The New Jim Crow*, a key component to the ever-growing calls for criminal justice reform, and even speaks holistically to the call for change in policing reform via the George Floyd murder and international movement of 2020. I have come to realize in my professional life as a social worker in public defender work and via other areas I've performed while in criminal justice that the answer to this question is a critical component deficient from many entities seeking to implement social, correctional, educational and therapeutic change with the historic and ever-present difficulties with at-risk minorities from historically oppressed cultures; particularly efforts to change the difficulties and major stronghold of African Americans as the largest proportional clientele in the American criminal justice system. Further, it speaks forward in ways how the criminal justice system can improve with other disparities (Hispanic Americans and Native Americans) and as a whole to find greater reform that truly tends toward true behavioral modification, public safety that is holistic and growing toward a definite end of historic disparities and collateral consequences of the American criminal justice system.

Further, no matter one's side on the issues of crime, punishment, corrections, and the rebirthed civil rights era brought about by the untimely murder of George Floyd (may I add a historic plague that has only become more visible via the continued rise of 24-7 technology and social media), the issues of this scene's importance are crucial if the call for "change" is to truly occur. Additionally, as the social unrest of the Floyd era shed international light on historic problems troubling inner cities and has reframed and reemphasized the need for criminal justice reform, the deeper implications of this scene need to be unpacked. If America is to change the plight of one of the ugliest stains from its "origin sin of racism," the disproportionate number of African Americans stuck in the shackles of the criminal justice system must be forever changed. This scene provides a major anchor toward holistic change with the criminal justice system that currently is not getting as much attention as other valid avenues with regards to criminal justice reform and the continued calls for racial justice and change, from the significant focus on the issue with the emphasis and laws passed by the Obama presidency, Trump presidency (yep, believe it or not, he did pass criminal justice reform legislation), and into the President Biden era and beyond.

How can this scene speak to the call for criminal justice reform and speak to the controversial dynamics of policing and crime? How can it assist with ending historic disparities in prisons and probation caseloads? How can it begin to reverse the impact of criminal justice collateral consequences that have been in effect since the days of slavery? What are the needed follow-ups and answers to the influence of Michelle Alexander's book, *The New Jim Crow: Mass Incarceration in the Age of Colorblindness*, Ava DuVernay's documentary *13th*, and many other noble endeavors to address these concerns? How do we bring about a holistic *Just Mercy* from lawyer Bryan Stevenson's book/movie and his greater work on equal justice initiatives? How do the policies of the past and present executive branch on police reform and criminal justice reform (not to mention other national and local leaders, too many to name) change the face of jails, prisons, courts, and probation caseloads? While there are many ways to go about this historic problem, and for that, it needs various efforts to change the criminal justice system. One focus needs better attention and can be pulled from this iconic television phenomenon. Simply but profoundly, Kunta Kinta was not only a name but an identity that went back lineages and inculcated all that this young man was and was to aspire to be. To relinquish that name was to relinquish who he was, a way of life, indeed a substantial piece of the totality of his humanity. Moreover, and much more impactful, it was to bring about a deep-rooted depression and future confusion of purpose and practicality.

This miniseries depicted the real-life saga of Alex Haley's family of origin. The beauty of the series was how this family was able to keep its identity through the many horrific and unjust ostracizes of American racism and slavery. As you weave your way through this miniseries (or book), you come to understand how the drama firmly depicts something far greater than the physical beatings and the slavery of human beings; it depicts the fight to not lose individual, cultural, and community self-worth. It shows the tremendous struggle, journey, and often loss that sheds a very important and descriptive light on many at-risk African Americans and other at-risk minorities that frequent the criminal justice system. This idea of holding on to cultural identity is at the crux of that matter.

Any simple gaze into American jails and prisons or even a brief Google of disparity statistics in the criminal justice system will show an overabundance of evidence of the age-old issue of minorities crowding the criminal justice system. Similarly, statistics that correlate with these crime statistics, such as educational disparities and vast social disparities, are well described and fashionably depicted in media and literature. In this day and age, it has become so normal that it's no longer shocking but assumed. Given the rebirth of considering the tragedy of police shootings of people of color, what hasn't been addressed is the cyclical system that all this occurs within and often grows from. Some would go so far as to say that people "bank" on these disparities in the criminal justice system and all its various outgrowths. Conspiracy theorists beware, as many believe these things are baked into the system so that the livelihood and sustenance of the majority culture are maintained and sustained or given vitality due to its ability to maintain a permanent underground or subculture that is dependent on the majority while being barred in an American caste system of sorts.

These statistical realities are so substantial that in the historic presidential election of November 2024, the Republican candidate for president of the United States thought he could appeal to African American voters because he was under numerous criminal indictments, of which he was convicted of 34 of those. In a campaign speech he tried to appeal to African Americans due to his criminal plight. He even alluded to a criminal mugshot for one of his indictments and its supposed similarity to the African American population, noting, “You know who embraced it [his mugshot] more than anyone else? The black population.”[1]

No matter the reasoning or whether the conspiracy theories are valid, while normality is locked on this issue of minorities in the criminal justice system and as America continues to try to address this problem, there is still a serious epidemic with at-risk minorities in the criminal justice system, African Americans being the greatest of those, as they represent 13 percent of the American population while representing 36 percent to 40 percent of prisons and jails in America. Residually, it speaks to consequent collateral consequences of generations and generations of these cultures in the criminal justice system. More concerning, amid the growth of evidence-based practices, the statistical lowering of crime, advancements in correctional practices, strength-based programming, and the data to back it, the criminal justice system, in its efforts to correct and rehabilitate, is failing at-risk minorities, and sadly failing its largest proportionate commodity and resource (yes, I did write that). A very morbid assertion, but unfortunately true, which we will unpack later. Moreover, decade after decade and at the expense of finding answers to these problems, nothing has dramatically dropped the statistics of African Americans in the criminal justice system.

Respective of the obvious issues, such as the rise of the 2020 era of police shootings, urban unrest, and its residual dynamics, the problem of overrun prisons and probation caseloads is a root of what is being seen in these ugly problems. While not getting the same amount of attention, the large disparity problem and curing that problem through paying attention to cultural identity is a key to changing the issue of disparities. It also lends knowledge to the problems of police shootings, the rise of police mistrust, and the continued problems in urban areas.

Alexander notes rhetorically in her previously mentioned book (a contemporary lexicon to the disparities in the criminal justice system) in an effort to push a bolder operation at changing disparities in prisons, "to really change this issue, America would have to release thousands of felons from its prisons."[2] To be fair, she elaborates how this wouldn't be possible and expounds on various other worthy avenues. Taking this profound idea to its full extent or even at a level many activists hope with contemporary ideas for criminal justice change, the outflow of this minimally being considered may yield surprising results. This is a hard truth not said much in America's discourse on the problem of inner cities, violent crime, and police shootings (get ready as it is harsh and does not link with political correctness or being "woke"), given the "one in three black men"[3] that will be in prison at some time in their lives, the fact is, prison and probation caseloads could be emptied and many of the same clients that have been owned by the criminal justice system would come back within its clutches. This is not an excuse to set aside the imbalanced practices that Black Lives Matter has highlighted and the lingering problems of America's historic racialized criminal justice system. But as this book will expound on, it is partly due to what Kunta Kinte did not want to give up: his cultural identity.

While the criminal justice system has been historically racist and still grapples with racist tendencies and while there are other issues that affect this problem, such as bad policing, the culture of poverty, the war on drugs, chemical health, mental health, lack of education, broken homes, and a lack of economic mobility. There is a continued but often ignored larger issue after decades of systematic racial issues and disproportionate incarceration and probation of minorities. That issue is that many at-risk minorities identify with criminality or, better, its sad collateral consequences as a part of their normality or have been forced to live in the box of this identity. Or many have psychologically settled within the crippling confines of incarceration and its collateral consequences as a normal part of their cultural lineage. With respect to the obvious issues all at-risk populations from historically oppressed cultures face and the traditional treatment, educational, social service-oriented, and corrective components necessary for optimum corrections and criminal justice, when it comes to the historic, disproportionate, and embedded culture of minorities in the criminal justice system, addressing the issue of identity from a cultural standpoint is a core issue that is overlooked in most traditional law enforcement, court, correctional and treatment programming, the totality of the criminal justice system. Moreover, it is a key component to the evolving thoughts and policies around criminal justice reform, if not a core foundation on which other components of reform should emanate

Under various terminology and philosophy, this idea of identity is not, in the least part, new, but it is not being addressed in the context of criminology and corrections. There is a cultural identity crisis with at-risk minorities and, specifically, a failure to address this aspect adequately within the criminal justice system. More specifically, it appears to be absent in practicality in correctional departments, probation caseloads, prisons, jails, correctional treatment/therapy, and government or policy-oriented efforts toward criminal justice and behavioral modification. This cultural identity crisis is an important barrier in the criminal justice system as it relates to treatment, rehabilitation, and corrective processes to assist with changing this weathered and deep-rooted culture of minorities in the criminal justice system. I boldly attest if this aspect of the journey toward change is ignored, our nation will continue to have disparities in jails and prisons. It is obviously imperative and understandable that the front-end efforts toward policies on policing, crime, urban unrest, and criminal justice reform are needed and will continue to be needed, and upon them, the notion of this logic stands, but these efforts alone will be fruitless if the system doesn't go deeper to the "Seeds of Toby," if you will, that has been embedded since the early days of America.

As typical efforts toward disparities, civil rights, advocacy, police shootings, urban crime, punishment, system change, corrections, and treatment focus on a front-end ideal (how African Americans or minorities got in the system and the ills that caused national disparities), there must be more attention on back-end issues, how to truly lower disparities, and get African Americans or minorities out of the system. That is the focus here, a holistic view and an understanding that many "George Floyd's" and otherwise that did not die at the knee of a police officer were damned and ushered into a horrible criminal justice system and collaterally stuck in keeping it in its clutches. Moreover, a system that seems to be refusing to adopt true cultural competency in its practices within a majority of criminal justice practices.

As will be divulged in this book, I contend that the back-end work is much more or at least just as crucial as a foundation to support all reform anchors. True criminal justice reform, true change (the "change" that the Floyd movement called for) must focus on among many dynamics, and among those dynamics, it should be a programmatic and policy-oriented emphasis on what I espouse as a cultural identity crisis that is partly at the root to disparities within the criminal justice system, and therefore, this issue must be proactively addressed in criminal justice structures. That is the purpose of this book.

To better empower minority at-risk populations beyond criminality and the unending roller coaster of the criminal justice system, there must be a better focus on a nontraditional and cultural treatment component that focuses on the identity paradigm of those engulfed in the criminal justice system. By identity paradigm, I mean the impact of a person's heritage, those dynamics that are passed down from preceding generations. Additionally, this is about a worldview by which a person acts and reacts, both positively and negatively. These crucial aspects are tattooed internally and ethnically on a person's emotional and psychological makeup and have a vast foundational effect on their mental health, outlook, and behavior.

The criminal justice system has recognized the need to change the thinking of clients within the system, and various theories are being used to assist in changing the aberrant mindset of those criminally active and incarcerated. With respect to these cognitive restructuring theories, such as *Thinking for a Change* and *True Thought*, many of these best practices and data-confirmed methods fall short of considering the cultural elements that are animated within the criminal mindset and behavior. In theory, the idea of cultural competence is always ruminated. It's a stylish thing to rehash at meetings, required trainings and policy-oriented efforts. But a few efforts take the necessary steps to see that culturally competent policies are implemented.

With a high consideration of the elements of the criminal justice system that need to change or upgrade, improper cultural identity paradigms and worldviews, in essence, one's cultural identity or ethnic racial identity is a chief aspect that is absent or fractured in the lives of those that frequent the criminal justice system and therefore the system must mandate that alternatives focus on this issue. While supportive of traditional programming and committed to its place in the criminal justice system, alternatives must begin to push clients to the positivity of their heritage and/or assist clients in creating a wholesome life focus that operates as a bedrock impetus for a productive and crime-free life.

This is particularly pivotal in the lives of youth and young adults. For minority youth and young adults, specifically from historically oppressed groups, this journey is colored by a cultural identity crisis where historical and contemporary residuals of racism play a significant part in forming their identity. In lieu of the critical stages of development for youth and young adults, this referencing is specifically pertinent to youth or youth adults who are at-risk or high-risk, and consequently, the negative side effects of this crisis are much more significant and must be understood and treated. Otherwise, many of these young adults will adopt an identity that routes their journey through the criminal justice system. For many of these precious young lives, recidivism and systematic social implications follow and cripple their lives into a spiral that is difficult to change.

The heartbreaking "one in three" black young men being destined to prison stat takes on new meaning seen in this way.

In consideration of this issue of a cultural identity crisis, is it valid? What is a cultural identity crisis and what are its implications for at-risk minorities? Can this thought have a definite impact on the criminal justice system? Can the epidemic of minorities in the criminal justice system be changed through additional concentration on this dynamic? Additionally, can this long-standing issue have an impact on the consequent, correlating, or collaborating issues in the social and educational arenas that stereotypically describe American at-risk minority cultures? This discourse will grapple with these issues and the theory's potential impact.

While focusing on all at-risk minority groups that are prevalent in the criminal justice system, this book will hypothesize the cultural identity crisis primarily through the view of the culture that is the proportionately largest in American jails and prisons, African Americans. These thoughts are considered transferable but highlighted best through the African American or the Native American journey. Given my professional expertise and personal culture as a black man, the African American dynamic will be highlighted as a foundation of this discourse, and it can be applied more largely to other historical disparities in the criminal justice system (Native Americans and Hispanic Americans).

In totality, the goals of this book are to challenge criminal justice system reform, the systems of correctional change, and other entities that naturally deal with the residuals of the criminal justice system, with the hopes of evolving the American criminal justice focus on treatment and rehabilitation. Second, this discourse will expound this idea of a cultural identity crisis with hopes of engendering or extracting further research and development on this identity notion with the focus of building a foundation for procedures and standards to assist with lowering the large amounts of minorities in the criminal justice system. This focus is also coupled with the passion to continue the *call to action* for criminal justice reform but add in a more holistic "call" directly and indirectly with individuals and entities in the criminal justice system to forever lower the disparities of minorities in the American criminal justice system.

Lastly, throughout this specific *call to action*, I will highlight my professional experience as a social worker in public defender work and my personal experience of growing up as an at-risk African American male to give practical context to these thoughts. Simply all told, the continued reality of disparities in criminal justice cannot continue if America is to fulfill its goal of "We the People," the idea of the American dream, and, if indeed, we can better move beyond the racial divide in our country. Following the *Seeds of Toby* can lead us toward these thoughts; we will glean from the growth it can produce.

PART 1

The Case for and More Evolved Look at Criminal Justice Reform

CHAPTER 1

The Continued Reality

As a public defender social worker who has worked in Minnesota, Arizona, and Colorado (this profession is also termed Sentencing Advocate, Mitigation Specialist, Mitigation Investigator, Forensic Social Worker, Capital Mitigation Specialist and Dispositional Advisor), and has worked in other fields in the criminal justice system (youth counselor, police officer, juvenile residential treatment supervisor), there have been many stories over my twenty-five years in criminal justice work that speaks to the significance of the notion of a cultural identity crisis and its practical implications in the criminal justice system. But none more significant than my work with a minority athletic star named Gene (fictional name). Gene was a great high school athlete who had collegiate and professional aspirations. Coupled with his aspirations was his qualified talent that began to open collegiate doors of opportunity. Despite his great talent, Gene came from a family of entrenched criminality, gang behavior, and family trauma. Amid these challenges, Gene was able to break away at times to be involved in high school sports.

As good as Gene was at sports, he was also that good at crime, which is so common to his family and surroundings. He found himself involved in various crimes that stunted his personal and athletic life. During this time, I and other criminal justice and court professionals were brought in to help Gene beyond his crime into a hopeful life of positivity. Gene was in the criminal justice system due to a felony-level crime and facing an adult sentence as a juvenile.

While working with Gene, I asked him a question to motivate him to be positive and away from a life of crime, "Do you know you can't get in the professional sports if you are involved in crime and gangs?" To my stunned amazement, Gene responded back to me with a snappy and witty comment that I will not soon forget. It was a comment that spoke profoundly of the stereotypical black athlete and the plight of what at-risk young African American teenagers often identify with. Gene answered me and said, "You know there are gangs and criminals in professional sports too!" This was said at a time when a handful of professional African American and Latin American athletes were highlighting the national news with gang behavior or alleged gang ties. While trying to respond to that comment the best I could, I knew I was stuck and couldn't adequately refute what he said. More importantly, as I later ruminated on his comments, I realized my attempt to use the "rags to riches" story of what sports could provide for him was little motivation to change his aberrant lifestyle and potentially supported his behavior currently.

Despite this challenge, we were able to get him into programming other than prison, which altered his life positively. Working with professionals on all sides of the criminal justice pendulum, including the prosecuting attorney, juvenile judge, and juvenile probation, we were able to get a lesser punishment for the crimes he was facing, averted an adult sentence, and got him into great juvenile residential treatment programming and reentry programming that supported his athletic talent and interests.

The judge presiding over this case placed him in a residential program far from his home where he was able to be away from his usual bad influences, and he consequently changed his behaviors, began to socialize with positive peers, continued to play high-level high school sports, solidified his opportunity to graduate high school and earned a college athletic scholarship. Gene was finally on the right track and became an example to use for other kids struggling with the same issues. It was exciting to see this progress, particularly in a field where what many would call success is rarely seen. All of the professionals who worked with Gene were excited to see the progress and looked forward to this young man breaking the chain of negativity of his upbringing.

Fast-forward, and you may already feel the progression of this story. Gene, while on the cusp of taking his life to another level, decided to change directions and become familiar with his old life of negativity. After he graduated from the juvenile residential program, he was placed in a specialized foster home to continue his schooling, life growth, and the athletics that led to his scholarship at a local college in the adjacent community. While things were seemingly going well, he decided to leave that foster home and all the anchors he had built for himself. He moved back home and around the negativity he was so familiar with. It was not soon after that Gene did not finish high school and began to again live in criminality that many thought he had overcome. Consequently, he found himself in jail, facing another felony charge and prison sentence that would alter the positive direction he had built for himself. Gene continued to have a major criminal justice presence despite the talents he had to take him out of criminal negativity. Gene continued to be in and out of prison.

Gene did plan to finish school and hopefully keep his sports scholarship; he truly desired to play athletics in college and professionally, and he had that unique physical talent to go far. What happened with Gene? Why did he not choose a potential life of positivity? Professionals from various disciplines might have different ideas as to why this happened, and there are various ideas to glean from this familiar criminal justice reality. Like my other colleagues, I was professionally discouraged given his potential, and all that was done to assist him, and yes, I wanted one of those rare great stories in this business. And perhaps hasty on my part, I didn't want to depend on my experience and training to facilitate an answer why. I wanted to know the answer from his own words. In the normal sequence of working with Gene and seeing him in and out of the criminal justice system, I had a chance to speak with him. In discussions with Gene and observing the culture he grew up in, it became somewhat clear to me why he chose to leave the program and come back home. He identified and felt more comfortable with his at-risk lifestyle than he did with his growing success. Indeed, he identified with the notion of the criminal pro-athlete, but more so, he felt much more comfortable with a life of crime and negativity than the prospect of doing something he loved and the positive life it was building for himself.

Professionals in similar fields know this type of story all too well and can splice it many ways as to why a young man like this chose a life of negativity instead of a life of positivity. My premise, among various conclusions that could be ascertained, is that he did not choose or stick with this newfound and positive life due to the problem I'm suggesting, which is a cultural identity crisis. Not only did he think he didn't have to change his lifestyle to continue in high-level sports, but he also believed criminality and its various residual outgrowths were normal, comfortable, and to some degree stereotypically glamorous for him. For him to step into a prosocial world and its various demands were unfamiliar to the at-risk minority culture he grew up in, and while he would have easily taken the athletics and gone to college, the route of disturbing what he called normal to get there, he could not fathom life beyond what he felt normal and comfortable.

Current statistics continue to reveal that there are many "Genes" in the criminal justice system. Not all are budding athletes, but many are minority men and women with great potential in various areas. African Americans have historically led in the percentage of the US population in jails and prisons, and they are still leading in this category, not to mention the unfortunate collateral consequences of being in jail and prison. Anyone familiar with American criminal justice work knows and perhaps is tired of the continued statistics that point to facts such as the previously mentioned "one in three" (some are now suggesting it's one in five) African American men will be in prison at some time in their lives. Such statistics are very familiar and have been conducted in research after research and study after study. For the purpose of this discourse, we will not have a thorough rehash of the obvious and overabundant statistics. However, as a foundation, it is necessary to establish the reality of the story I just spoke to and, later, how focusing on this cultural identity crisis within the criminal justice system can change such statistics.

Given the pivotal moment that the George Floyd and social change era sparked in 2020, it is interesting to look at this issue prior to 2020 and after 2020. There were ebbs and flows of crime and criminal justice-related issues within the mid-2000s and given a thorough look at a historical issue that has been with the United States since the dawn of its history, with pivotal points just after 1864s abolishment of slavery, the civil rights movement of the 1960s and very contemporary and powerful to this issue, the tough on crime era of the 1990s, the 2020s are proving to be a landmark time of wanted change and/or substantiating yet again the need for criminal justice system change. Just years of the George Floyd, the verdict is out on what this landmark era will be or become.

The following statistics give a reminder of this historical issue and its view after George Floyd. While some changes have slightly emerged, it is a proverbial "throwing gas on the fire" of the disparities problem in the criminal justice system of America.

Before George Floyd

- *The National Council on Crime and Delinquency (NCCD)* states, "In the US, African Americans are over six times as likely to be incarcerated as whites; Latinos over twice as likely. If the US enacted the reforms necessary to reduce its disproportionate minority confinement by just 50%, the incarceration rate would drop…and put the US fifth in the world instead of first."[4]
- *National Association for the Advancement of Colored People (NAACP)* states that the majority of the 2.3 million people incarcerated in US prisons and jails are people of color, people with mental health issues and drug addiction, people with low levels of educational attainment, and people with a history of unemployment or underemployment.[5]
- *Report of the Sentencing Project to the United Nation Human Rights Committee*: One in every three black males born today can expect to go to prison at some point in their life, compared with one in every six Latino males and one in every seventeen white males, if current incarceration trends continue.[6]
- *The Center for American Progress, "The Top 10 Most Startling Facts About People of Color and Criminal Justice in the United States"*

1. While people of color make up about *30 percent* of the United States population, they account for *60 percent* of those imprisoned.
2. According to the Bureau of Justice Statistics, *one in three black men* can expect to go to prison in their lifetime.
3. Students of color face harsher punishments in school than their white peers, leading to a higher number of youth of color incarcerated.
4. According to recent data by the Department of Education, African American students are arrested far more often than their white classmates.
5. African American youth have higher rates of juvenile incarceration and are more likely to be sentenced to adult prison.
6. As the number of women incarcerated has increased by *800 percent* over the last three decades, *women of color have been disproportionately represented.*
7. The war on drugs has been waged primarily in communities of color where people of color are more likely to receive higher offenses.
8. Once convicted, black offenders receive longer sentences compared to white offenders.
9. Voter laws that prohibit people with felony convictions to vote disproportionately impact men of color.
10. Studies have shown that people of color face *disparities in wage trajectory* following release from prison.[7]

- *The Sentencing Project report, The Color of Justice: Racial and Ethnic Disparities in State Prisons, Key Findings.*

    - African Americans are incarcerated in state prisons at a rate that is 5.1 times the imprisonment of whites. In five states (Iowa, Minnesota, New Jersey, Vermont, and Wisconsin), the disparity is more than ten to one.
    - In twelve states, more than half of the prison population is black: Alabama, Delaware, Georgia, Illinois,

Louisiana, Maryland, Michigan, Mississippi, New Jersey, North Carolina, South Carolina, and Virginia. Maryland, whose prison population is 72 percent African American, tops the nation.

- In eleven states, at least one in twenty adult black males is in prison.
- In Oklahoma, the state with the highest overall black incarceration rate, one in fifteen black males ages eighteen and older is in prison.
- States exhibit substantial variation in the range of racial disparity, from a black/white ratio of 12.2:1 in New Jersey to 2.4:1 in Hawaii.
- Latinos are imprisoned at a rate that is 1.4 times the rate of whites. Hispanic/white ethnic disparities are particularly high in states such as Massachusetts (4.3:1), Connecticut (3.9:1), Pennsylvania (3.3:1), and New York (3.1:1).[8]

The big picture of this continued reality is found in the following statistics with support of the 2019 Bureau of Justice Statistics. With the previously mentioned statistics and the big picture of the United States, the issue in context becomes much more disturbing and concerning:

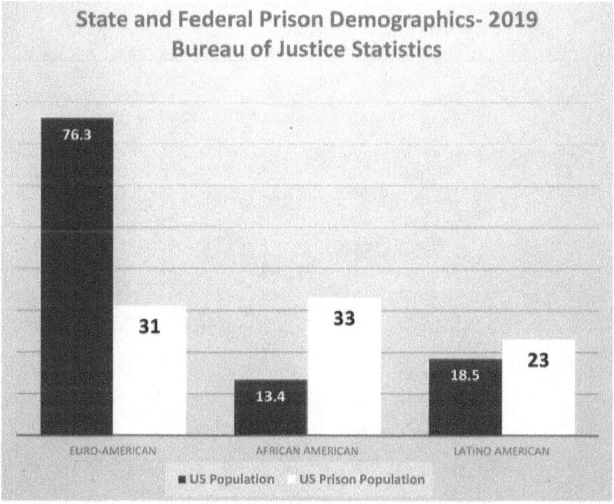

9

The Pew Research Center and the Prison Policy Initiative show similar totals in their statistics:

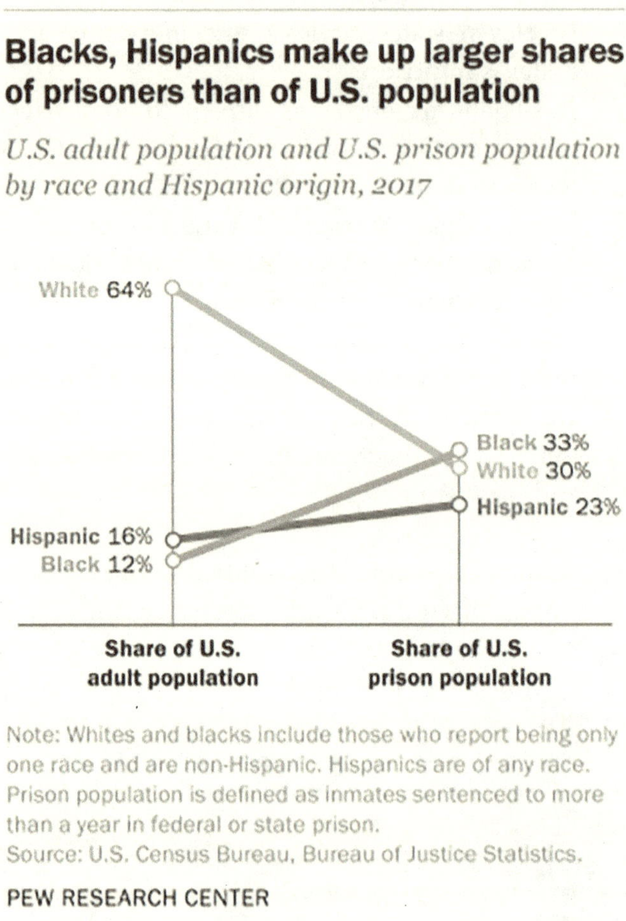

[10]

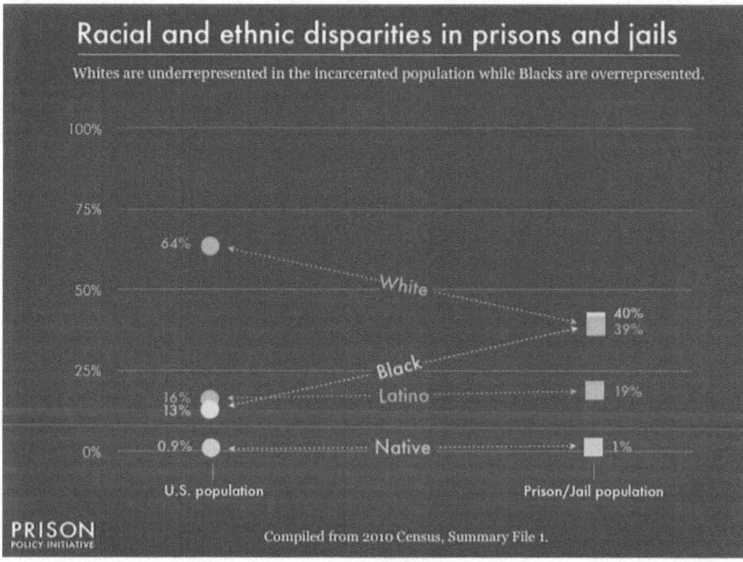

[11]

After George Floyd

- *Bureau of Justice Statistics, Prisoners in 2022—Statistical Tables*: "A t yearend 2022, an estimated 32% of sentenced state and federal prisoners were black; 31% were white; 23% were Hispanic; 2% were American Indian or Alaska Native; and 1% were Asian, Native Hawaiian, or Other Pacific Islander."[12]
- *The Sentencing Project, One in Five: How Mass Incarceration Deepens Inequality and Harms Public Safety*: "While all major racial and ethnic groups experienced decarceration, the Black prison population has downsized the most.4 But with the prison population in 2022 nearly six times as large as 50 years ago and Black Americans still imprisoned at nearly five times the rate of whites, the crisis of mass incarceration and its racial injustice remain undeniable."[13]

- *The Pew Center Research, Racial Disparities Persist in Many US Jails*:

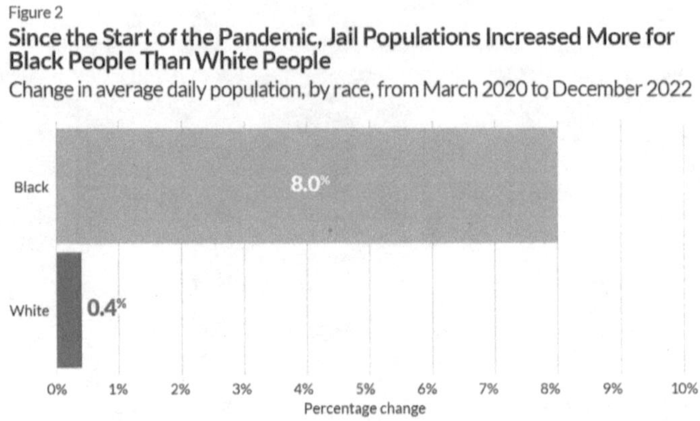

14

- *The Prison Policy Initiative, Mass Incarceration: The Whole Pie 2024*: "It's no surprise that people of color—who face much greater rates of poverty—are dramatically overrepresented in the nation's prisons and jails. These racial disparities are particularly stark for Black Americans, who make up 35% of the prison and jail populations but only 14% of all US residents."

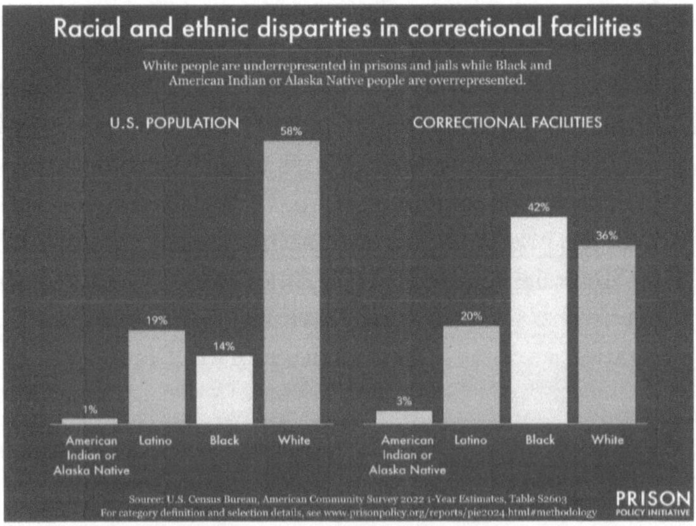

15

The reports and statistics go on and on with substantial study after study. These are the hard facts, and seemingly, in the research world, it is trendy to publish the latest and same conclusions about the criminal justice system. While there have been drops in crime and minimal change has occurred with disparities, this is the continued reality that has been repeating itself historically. It sheds light on the continued reality of racism or the remnants of racism. Some scoff when it is said that the criminal justice system is racist, but if you look at it in the context of these repeated and historic statistics, how then shall you conclude?

At the beginning of the historic Obama era, many thought we were living or growing into a post-racial America, given the US voted in its first minority and African American president, and further, a brilliant leader who embraced diversity, equity, and equality. Now years in review, the US obviously still struggles as it saw the tragedies highlighted from Trayvon Martin to George Floyd and beyond. Race and racism are still a mammoth factor in the American way of life. To be sure, America has come a long way. I can boldly attest to this as an African American from my generation that lives even better than those in my parents and grandparents' generations. Yes, America has evolved and is a better place to live racially. However, the US is still catastrophically struggling, and, in my opinion, the epicenter of today's racism is the criminal justice system because it is one entity that is stubborn and truncated in old ways of looking at crime and punishment, and more importantly it has long-lasting collateral consequences externally and internally. While America is better, no culture can truly flourish in the realms of America's promise when such statistics describe a high percentage of its people. The sociological or psychological collateral consequences or the residual impact of historic incarceration alone is a weight too much to bear. It is crippling and indeed cripples America as a whole.

These issues alone brought America to the 2020 rebirth of the civil rights era or just brought the continuing and ever-present movement to light again. That specific movement was reignited to challenge these overbearing statistics of disproportionality exemplified in the extinguishing of precious lives through police violence. But did it go far enough to address the issues it was passionate about? A bigger question is and a topic for another discussion: Did it already fade away without making its intended change?

As will be discussed throughout this book and with a continued support of advocacy and activism for the frontline concerns for law enforcement and criminal justice reform, the goal is to rethink or think deeper about today's issues of race and the criminal justice system and hopefully motivate thoughts and maybe different or more holistic actions and reactions to these serious problems. Think about these various statistics; in fact, google your own study and different resources. With such statistics, how then should we look at these extremely tense issues? Is it just bad policing and laws that continue these large disparities in jails and prisons?

For sure, there is a need for continued valiant front-end advocacy, such as the mentioned police reform, or a continued change in the drug laws from the "war on drugs" era, upgrading or eliminating unjust bail systems, clemency, changing disproportionate discipline of minority youth in schools (the School to Prison Pipeline), fairness in jury selection, diversifying police forces and other common issues in the struggle for equity in the justice system. But what about ideas around corrections reform and transformative and bold ideas that go beyond POTUS Obama's push to change solitary confinement and bolster reentry programming efforts,[16] POTUS Trump's corrections policies with his passage of the First Step Act,[17] or POTUS Biden's attempts at The George Floyd Justice in Policing Act[18] and the various attempts after these national efforts bring about criminal justice reform? What additional ideas can substantially assist in changing the historical impact of a system that has overridden African Americans and other minorities since the birth of the United States of America?

We cannot forget that there are still many lives in prison today. If the "one in three" statistic holds, there will continue to be large disparities in jails and prisons. There are still many lives that were in prison that are now impacted by what prison did or didn't do too/for mom's, dad's, families and residually halted or even stopped opportunities for economic, educational, and psychological health. Indeed, such basics as having a job, a nice home to live in, or the ability to vote.

As spoken to previously, and while applauding the movement of reform, it's my opinion that was changing front-end or frontline issues or how people get in jail and prison is only one part of what is needed, and if left alone, it will not change disparities drastically. Perceive the events from Trayvon Martin to George Floyd and beyond through a deeper lens, and you'll see a greater work to do than what is currently espoused. Consider not only the external impact of *The New Jim Crow* but also the internal impact (psychological, emotional, familial, social, spiritual) of this historical burden on a culture since it stepped on the shores of America.

As many of America's urban cities often get press for the continued violence of their communities and overemphasized in political campaigns, step back on what seems obvious and think if the statistics are correct, incarceration is a negative theme that is woven throughout those communities and historically, mind you. Quite simply, in today's American criminal justice system and given its vast historical and contemporary collateral consequences and, to this book's point, its stubbornness to become culturally competent, the American criminal justice system is still a powerful arm of racism and the last and most ardent systematic and historical weight of racism in America. I would argue that because of its ability not only to restrict freedom physically but, even more impactful, its ability to restrict freedom internally and psychologically. Moreover, all efforts toward criminal justice reform must look both inwardly and outwardly if the goal is success. While there is momentum toward the change of outward and overt failures of the criminal justice system, momentum must continue to evolve to work on addressing internal psychological and cultural dynamics that challenge the identity and consequent continued lifestyles of the lives it disproportionately incarcerates.

CHAPTER 2

The Last Leg of Expansive Systematic Racism

Working within court systems, I see much of what we typically hear about on TV or the social media airwaves about injustice within the criminal justice system. It is vivid, and it is real. There are various dynamics in the justice system that need to be changed. There is an imbalance, and there are inequities. Whether its issues revolve around the need for policing reform or equal justice under the law, it is still truncated in the American criminal justice system. As I've noted and support wholeheartedly, there does need to be a continued focus on front-line issues that speak to how people get into the criminal justice system.

One such case I was assigned to work on in my role as a public defender work was a criminal vehicle homicide case. At the onset, I must express that I believe in the final analysis that justice was served, but the greater perspective of what I experienced with this case and another similar case shed light on the issues that can become discouraging and divisive. As I describe this story and others, obvious specific details will be left out, but the general facts and consensus of these stories will be noted.

In many respects, this case was typically tragic of what is seen in these situations. A young man, in this case, a young adult male in his early twenties, African American, was out late with friends. He and his friends were consuming drugs and drinking alcohol. He decides to get into a car and presumably drive home while impaired by his chemical abuse. He gets in his car, and as he was driving, this young man misses the stop light and proceeds to hit a Euro-American young lady and kill her. This young lady was amazing and had a great future, and this was brought out in the court process. Without question, this was a horrible situation and, most importantly, the tragic loss of a beautiful life.

Within my capacity as a public defender, social worker, and mitigation specialist, I was brought in to assist with the defense and, in my capacity, assure that the best legal outcomes would come about at sentencing. In this regard, from a social work framework, I studied the defendant's risk factors and protective factors: his family history, past criminal record, school records, treatment records, significant life dynamics, and current mental health, all in accordance with the case and its legal ramifications. This client was in jail with a bail tremendously too high to get out of jail while his case continued, and thus, all my meetings and work with the client were in a jail setting.

To expound a little better as to my role, for those in the probation or parole business, you are familiar with what is called a presentencing investigation/report, PSI or PSR. This document is used by probation to determine appropriate sentencing for a defendant by reviewing the client's life dynamics and then assessing criminal risk factors or predictions. Then this document is submitted to the court to assist with sentencing outcomes from a corrections or probation standpoint. My role from a defense perspective, in this case, was to do the same, but from a legal defense perspective, I would suggest it in a more holistic fashion. Basically, the other side of the criminal justice system sought balance in all aspects of the case.

As such, from my study and work, we were seeking a lesser time in prison than state guidelines proposed, with the addition that the defendant, this African American young man, be immersed in a year-long chemical residency program. As you can imagine, this was not the sentiment of the prosecuting attorney nor the probation department. As I will detail later, another part of my job is to find root causes of behavior and, consequently, effective programming that will address that behavior hopefully more effectively than prison. In the case of true public safety and lowering recidivism, that could be prison, a therapeutic alternative, or a combination of both. Hence, the recommendation of a residential chemical dependency program to work on the primary problem or cause of the behavior of this client: chemical dependency. Within that context of the case, as you can further imagine, this case garnered media attention. This was no surprise at all, given the magnitude of the case.

After all our work on behalf of the case, the sentencing hearing came, and it was a display of justice in work and, in this case, toward a proper outcome although my position and recommendation were for this idea of year-long chemical dependency program. The sentencing was very emotional to the place where even the judge presiding over the sentencing was in tears. Consequently, on the merits, this young man was sent to prison without a lessened or altered sentence, and without the chemical dependency program we pushed for. It was a just and proper outcome of the case although I disagreed because my client's chemical dependency issues would not be addressed in prison.

Prior to this sentencing, I met with our client various times in preparation for the case. As I met with this young man, as I almost always do in this work, I saw a real young man that made a mistake. I saw a promising and gifted young man with the potential to be very successful. But as well, I experienced a young man that was struggling with the psychological terror of his offense. Additionally, a young man whose life patterns had been the subject of what some would term at-risk or high-risk. Unfortunately, he was becoming one of these "one in three" black males who go to prison, and his past and current legal plight fit many of the stereotypes. What was very interesting about this was that this young man expressed to me how it angered him that he would now be looked at that way, being another African American man in the criminal justice system, and while understanding his mistake, he didn't want to be perceived in the negative stereotypes of African American men in jail and prison.

Now this does not end here as you might think. Some months later, I received another similar case. However, this time, the individual that caused the tragic harm was a Euro-American lady who was intoxicated and ended up killing another innocent life, yes, a darling of a Euro-American young lady with again an amazing life and future ahead of her.

In my work with this client, the same focus as the previous client, I met her in my office as she was not in custody, which was significant. In fact, she was from another state and had the ability to travel to and from for her legal proceedings. Now in criminal justice work, no two cases are exactly alike, and many times, it depends on the judges, attorneys, the county, the state, and so on to see how things practically shake out. But I need to go no further, in that even as this case was beginning to play out, the reaction to the same type of tragic loss was different in the same area and state but with a different context with regards to who was the victim and victimizer. The defendant in this case did go to prison for a much smaller amount of time than in the former case, and the process and outcome treated her very differently and with a lesser time committed to prison.

Such scenarios are typical and rightfully need examination and change for equitable outcomes. This seems unjust as it was played out in two different scenarios but within miles of each other and within the same state. Add in the various national stories of police brutality, uneven court trials, and the previously noted disparities running amuck throughout America. These circumstances have been unbearable for a large part of American history. But I want to challenge the discourse to go a little deeper. While these scenarios are deeply concerning, racism and its grip on the criminal justice system is much deeper than battling these obvious problems. Further, there needs to be a paradigm shift if we want to get at the root of the issues of disparities and see real change with overabundant issues we are seeing with race and the criminal justice system.

When working, I enter the jails, prisons, courtrooms, meetings, conferences, and committees on behalf of my clients. It is no surprise that I'm one of few minorities, and certainly African Americans, that are in a role of leadership to assist with a highly diverse clientele. Nothing is more astonishing and oddly amazing than walking into jails and prisons. If you can imagine myself, a dark chocolate man, clad in suit and tie, walks into a jail to conduct business with his clients. When I go through various security checks and locked doors, I come into the designated areas to meet my clients, and as I look in, I see a colony of African American men as the panoramic backdrop of all the detainees within the walls of jail. Conversely, it could be a majority of Latino men, which is just as startling. These men stare at me in amazement because of the oddity of a "brotha," a black man, being on the other side, among other similar thoughts. I also stare in amazement (inwardly) with a consistent double-take on the diversity within jail or prison populations juxtaposed to what I see in courts with my client and I, often being the only minorities. Although I've been in these scenarios thousands of times with my work, even still, it is a gaze of bewilderment at milieu after milieu of the heavy presence of minority Americans under lock, key, and command of a system built to incarcerate and "correct" behavior.

No disrespect to my various correctional colleagues, but imagine and take yourself back to pre-1863. This remarkably equates in view of what I assume slavery looked like before my time. Good, bad, ugly, or just the system at work "keeping the community safe," the scene of African Americans being watched over, commanded, and in shackles in mass is a demoralizing and vivid sight. This issue is continually startling, particularly when some communities outside of the jail and courts and people hired to deal with all manner of issues related to the incarcerated barely represent the diversity inside these prisons and jails.

The previously mentioned statistics reveal this all across America. Scores and scores of black men and brown men are shackled by the criminal justice system. It is a very tragic scene and residual mess when you consider how deeply this process dovetails into various aspects of American life, none more seriously than the rebirth of a global civil rights movement sparked by the murder of George Floyd, not to mention the vast health inequities revealed via the COVID-19 pandemic of 2020.

Historic Intentionality

These tragic scenes are at the American forefront every day. I've been privileged to train and present in representation of these issues nationally, and while there's a difference, this issue is continual throughout America as I've witnessed it. While past, at least in our view, and seemingly somewhat forgotten nationally, just the thought that the criminal justice system brought America back to a civil rights era of modern times should continue to wake America up to this bold notion, the American criminal justice system is the last leg of expansive systematic racism of our past. Current and historical statistics alone visually send a message that something is wrong and has been wrong for decades and centuries. But stats alone, I will admit, do not prove or tell the full story. One reason why these statements so boldly roll from my tongue and are discussed in this book is because of the historic intentionality that keep this issue vibrant in America.

As mentioned, important prerequisites or additional research and discussion to this book are the great works of many people above my paygrade, above my intelligence, and are true trailblazers of this journey. Michelle Alexander and her cutting-edge book *The New Jim Crow: Mass Incarceration in the Age of Colorblindness*, Ava DuVernay's Netflix documentary, *13th*, and the vast work of Bryan Stevenson, to name just a few. Among many others and very well-researched documents and documentaries, these people and their works give a great foundation as to the intentionality throughout history in using the criminal justice system to enact racism over African Americans and other historically oppressed cultures in America. Many have spoken to these realities from other scholars and musicians. The hip-hop genre has made it a theme to movies and poems. Again, as the statistics reveal, something is clearly amiss if you have a population of people who represent 13 percent of the country yet occupy almost 40 percent of its jails and prisons, African Americans. These patterns are also averse with Native Americans, and the patterns are consistent with Latino Americans.

Not only do these resources speak to history, but they also display a compelling argument about contemporary measures to use criminal justice to enact racist policies and practical measures. Admittedly, I have not thoroughly ruminated deep into the idea of a continued conspiracy theory. My half-full nature bucks up against this idea. But some hold to the idea that this intentionality is so embedded that careers and economies depend on incarceration rates, and the fact that a huge chunk of that is depending on minority populations incarcerated. This is a consistent underpinning in regard to the privatization of jails, prisons, and corrections work. Also, it is a consistent thought about the boom of prisons being built in rural communities. National expert on prisons, Tracy Huling, noted in her report, *Building a Prison Economy in Rural America*, a quote against building prisons in rural America highlights this thought, "Beyond the obvious parallels that we are once again using black bodies to sustain white rural economies; we are setting ourselves up, over the long term, for greater racial tensions in this country."[19]

She further notes in this 2002 report almost a foreshadowing of what we have seen in America during the 2020s and beyond,

> The shockwaves of the prison-building spree in rural America are now penetrating the inner core of our nation's large cities and threatening dramatic and troubling changes in the way the nation allocates resources and political representation… The big losers in this shift will be urban communities of color. Half of all US prisoners are African American, and one-sixth are Latino.

This idea of a conspiracy theory of sorts or an economic purpose of incarceration throughout America is not an argument I seek to prove or debate. It's an issue that stands in its own thought and research. However, it highlights this idea of intentionality. It highlights the massive impact of incarceration and what will be further developed.

The historic intentionality of racist tendencies within law enforcement, courts, and the criminal justice system as a whole stands alone. Debates can rage, think tanks can muse, and research after research can be produced, but there is no denying its history and its current residual impact, and yes, some systems continue to be racist in criminal justice practice knowingly. Or perhaps even more scary, it's so rooted in criminal justice system history and America as a whole it's barely felt because it's that normal to our American way of life. Sickening, if so. As mentioned earlier, activism and advocacy need to enthusiastically continue to change this negativity, this intentionality. Further, upon this historic intentionality, this discourse stands and will evolve.

Collateral Consequences Legacy

Second, and a best friend to the previous notion of historic intentionality and much more impactful, is that America has experienced this historic intentionality so long, centuries even; there are historic "collateral consequences" of the impact of the centuries of the overcast via criminal justice. This dynamic exhibits much more of the substantial leg of racism than its overt and infamous partner, historic intentionality.

In context, what are collateral consequences, and why are they so important and impactful? Crime and imprisonment bring about natural and intended or systematic consequences, and that is to be expected. "When you do the crime, you do the time," as the saying goes. This can mean natural consequences. That could be guilt, social ostracization, or a loss of trust or privileges from the one offended. Then there are the intended or systematic consequences that society imposes on an offender, punitive measures, such as the ability to vote, an inability to get certain jobs, loss of gun privileges, and so on. My position is not that there should not be consequences for crimes; any functional and successful society will have punitive outcomes for criminal behavior. However, collateral consequences are criminal justice phraseology that speaks to the unfortunate and overreaching direct and indirect consequences that come about personally, socially, and civically to an individual after imprisonment or conviction of a crime. These consequences are often insurmountable barriers that many felons find very difficult to overcome, even if a felon has fulfilled their prison and probation sentences. In effect, "doing the time" means much more than state and federal spending time in prison.

Sarah Berson of the National Institute of Justice gives great perspective and meaning to the idea of collateral consequences:

> The consequences of a criminal conviction don't end with the prison sentence served or fines paid. Collateral consequences—separate from and in addition to direct consequences, such as imprisonment, fines and community supervision continue to affect millions of Americans who have been convicted of a crime as they attempt to develop productive lives after their release and rehabilitation.[20]

These consequences can include various dynamics, such as the inability to get a job, find a decent place to stay, education, and additional voting/civic restrictions. It also includes deeper aspects, such as mental health, social challenges, and societal and psychological strains. These consequences are additional and impact recidivism and a felon's ability to prosocially reenter society and be successful beyond crime. It includes the stigma of a prison record, the proverbial and contemporary "Scarlett Letter" that society puts on a person, and its often-ugly stereotypes guide the community in how it reacts to a former felon.

The intense crucible of collateral consequences is mammoth. It is well depicted in the infamous Oscar-nominated movie *Shawshank Redemption*, where among its various themes is this idea around long-time inmate Brooks Hatlen. Brooks, in this movie set in a 1950s prison, has served a fifty-year prison sentence and is now in good health but elderly. One key scene depicts him coming to the end of his prison sentence and the parole board deciding that he is to be now released from prison. After this decision, a sullen Brooks is shown upon announcement of his release and completion of his prison sentence, appearing puzzled and discouraged.

Brooks is so used to prison life he can't imagine living without the odd but consistent comforts that prison has provided for him. Before he leaves the prison, he describes this bewilderment to his inmate family, and they seek to console him. In sequence with this portion of the movie, Brooks leaves prison, gets a decent place to stay, a good first job at a grocery store, and begins to start his life anew. However, the pressure and lack of familiarity with the real world overcomes him so much he decides to hang himself, and he dies. This thematic presentation displays a psychological collateral consequence of prison, equating to another common phraseology in the criminal justice world, "institutionalization".

Collateral consequences have been so substantial various organizations and studies have developed research to focus on this problem. This movement has been under the guise of a dynamic called *reentry* and has produced programs focused on helping the "Brook Hatlens" of the world to reenter society successfully. Thus, helping individuals seeking to overcome its tremendous impact post-prison life.

As much as this is a major issue for those coming out of prison individually, contemplate how this can and has impacted a culture of people collectively for centuries. Review the statistics previously quoted, then multiply that over the duration of America's existence. Then think of not only individuals impacted by imprisonment, but also families, communities, and cultures becoming conglomerates Brooks Hatlens and a collective collateral consequence on generations. If taken in full view, the picture of incarceration under the notion of pre–civil rights totals and the last leg of historic racism is justifiably animated at a whole different level.

Jailed or imprisoned correctly or not (for the sake of argument), the historic incarceration of black men from the start of America has impacted the African American culture financially and educationally within its familial structures, its health, its mental health, its worldview, and its psychological well-being. Think of the impact this has had on Native Americans. How about Latino Americans? Then again, as asked before, think about all the racial issues and the cross-section of criminal justice and contemporary societal dynamics. For certain, this gives a broader look at a problem that extends to various contemporary issues that have been highlighted in the media in recent years.

With respect to this focus, there are two areas that are great examples of holistic collateral consequences of imprisonment on cultures. One is in the obvious area of an economic impact. Many professionals with competent research would conclude that "the culture of poverty" is a main antecedent to imprisonment. That is a valid notion, without question. Nevertheless, I would suggest in today's society imprisonment is a precursor to poverty. Worthy debate, but there is no question that the two unfortunate dynamic forces are powerfully linked. The Pew Center Trusts, in their report, *Collateral Costs: Incarceration's Effect on Economic Mobility*, shed light on how incarceration impacts a culture:

1. Incarceration Is Concentrated among Men, the Young, the Uneducated, and Racial and Ethnic Minorities—Especially African Americans.
    - One in eighty-seven working-aged white men is in prison or jail, compared with one in thirty-six Hispanic men and one in twelve African American men.
    - More young (twenty- to thirty-four-year-old) African American men without a high school diploma or GED are currently behind bars (37 percent) than employed (26 percent).

2. Incarceration Negatively Affects Former Inmates' Economic Prospects.
    - Serving time reduces hourly wages for men by approximately 11 percent, annual employment by nine weeks, and annual earnings by 40 percent.
    - By age forty-eight, the typical former inmate will have earned $179,000 less than if he had never been incarcerated.
    - Incarceration depresses the total earnings of white males by two percent, of Hispanic males by six percent, and of black males by 9 percent.

3. Former Inmates Experience Less Upward Economic Mobility Than Those Who Are Never Incarcerated.
   - Of the former inmates who were in the lowest fifth of the male earnings distribution in 1986, two-thirds remained on the bottom rung in 2006, twice the number of those who were not incarcerated.
   - Only 2 percent of previously incarcerated men who started in the bottom fifth of the earnings distribution made it to the top fifth twenty years later, compared to 15 percent of men who started at the bottom but were never incarcerated.

4. The Impacts of Incarceration Reach Far Beyond Former Inmates to Their Children and Families.
   - Fifty-four percent of inmates are parents with minor children (ages zero to seventeen), including more than 120,000 mothers and 1.1 million fathers.
   - About 2.7 million children have a parent behind bars—1 in every 28 children (3.6 percent) has a parent incarcerated, up from 1 in 125 just 25 years ago. Two-thirds of these children's parents were incarcerated for non-violent offenses.
   - One in nine African American children (11.4 percent), one in twenty-eight Hispanic children (3.5 percent), and one in fifty-seven white children (1.8 percent) have an incarcerated parent.

5. A Child's Prospect of Upward Economic Mobility Is Negatively Affected by the Incarceration of a Parent.
   - Previous research has shown that having a parent incarcerated hurts children, both educationally and financially.
   - Children with fathers who have been incarcerated are significantly more likely than other children to be expelled or suspended from school (23 percent compared with 4 percent).

- Family income averaged over the years a father is incarcerated is 22 percent lower than family income was the year before a father is incarcerated. Even in the year after the father is released, family income remains 15 percent lower than it was the year before incarceration. Both education and parental income are strong indicators of children's future economic mobility.[21]

Another well-documented area of holistic collateral consequence on cultures is in the area of education. Here, we will see the "which came first, the chicken or the egg" scenario. There are amazing studies speaking on this such as the infamous "school to prison to pipeline" studies and "the achievement gap" concept and the resultant various studies and commentaries on these issues. Statistics show that many of the incarcerated are educated minimally, most without a high school diploma. Lack of education and prison go hand in hand. However, from a historical or sociological standpoint, I would again argue that the historical impact of incarceration has played a more long-lasting impact on the role of education and its importance in African American communities than the reverse. Meaning, imprisonment has had such an impact, it has hurt the wealth of what education can do to people, families, and cultures. Regardless, there is no question about the unfortunate linkage between the aspects of low education and high imprisonment in American life.[22]

Understandably, this speaks to the idea that an incarcerated parent has an expediential impact and their children's education, but dynamic can impact the totality of a child's life. This includes a child's emotional, physical, educational, and financial well-being.[23] Given the previously quoted statistics on disproportionality and disparities, consider how that impacts a culture of people over decades.

The impact of incarceration has been resoundingly massive, at lengths we fear to unpack because getting back to the discussions of *The New Jim Crow* or the *13th* documentary. The presumed guilt of this nation would be far-reaching, leaning toward such controversial concepts of "reparations." For the purposes of this dialogue, the goal is not to rehash or debate legitimate and, in some cases, overworked arguments and movements. I attest again to many of these movements standing strong on their own. Moreover, this is not about understanding the conspiracy of historic incarceration of African Americans or exposing a racist criminal justice system again on the merits I believe that loudly speaks for itself. But if a lack of political correctness or being "woke" could allow America to say this, it would probably exclaim on these issues and obvious statistics loud and collective, "We get it already!" To that, I would say touché, and moreover, what is key for this dialogue is what is even more tragic beyond that is what does America do about the historic intentionality and collateral consequences of the criminal justice system? What does it do about the historical disparities in the American criminal justice system? While it is just as important to advocate and battle for social change, criminal justice reform, and better policing, I believe it is just as or perhaps much more important to work on the "what next" and build an understanding of deeper issues and consequences of these ugly realities. There must be an evolved focus on identity and consequent behavior. Then build bridges toward a concept away from a life of incarceration and its residual consequences. If mindsets do not change that have been historically planted due to the trauma of historic imprisonment, America will continue to deal with disparity issues within the criminal justice system, and I would debate the large front-end issues discussed earlier.

In my professional opinion, and while there are many other avenues to deal with racism and given the many things we've unfortunately experienced in recent years with race and its practical outcomes, disparities in the criminal justice system are "driving the bus" contemporarily and truly is the last leg of expansive historical racism in America. While changing law enforcement practices, court processes, probation practices, and closing prisons would be good and are drastically needed. While digging deeper into holistic concepts of the culture of poverty and the achievement gap would provide a great platform for change and need. While the criminal justice reform started by POTUS Obama, further developed under POTUS Trump and POTUS Biden, appears to have momentum forward and no doubt needed. And while America has a great watchful eye on procedures/policies to deal with bad policing, bad sentencing, and other issues of why minorities overwhelm the criminal justice system. For the sake of this argument, even if we released many of the wrongfully imprisoned minority young men and women and upgraded police policy to change bad policing and unrest in urban cities, there still must be a policy-oriented, programmatic, and therapeutic-oriented wave in jails, prisons, and probation caseloads and courts that focus on a deeper aspect if America wants true criminal justice reform. Not to mention, the cosmic shift is needed in the race discussion and its damaging consequences. I would attest this additional focus lies in unpacking deeper and more holistic issues such as historical trauma and positive identity development in lieu of the historic and extreme weight of the historic intentionality and collateral consequences the American criminal justice has heaped on minority Americans.

CHAPTER 3

An Unfortunate Truth about Black Lives Matter and Unrest in Urban Cities

While I grew up in surroundings that were, shall we say, stereotypical of what we would describe as a midwestern urban or inner-city life, up until 1992, it was all normal stuff, "how we rolled." I would say that for the racism I saw as well, horrible, but ya know, that's how it was. You fought what you could and adjusted otherwise. But in 1992, it was on, and this year became the first time I truly connected my ethnicity and culture with a racism that was vivid, historic, systematic, viral and full of seemingly insurmountable impact. It was the first time with a mature understanding I saw the original sin of slavery and its curse on America in a real time way. Moreover, for me, while stunned for a bit the first time, I really grappled within myself the need to be a change agent of some sort. For all intents and purposes, this year became, respectfully said with honor to the fallen and its requisite national and international movement, the George Floyd before the real George Floyd for me.

In 1992, I was on break sitting in a work lounge in downtown Indianapolis. I was about two years into college but now at home working, seeking to get more money to support my college habit. While I was sitting there, I saw on the TV the 1992 Los Angeles riots coverage and footage, the Rodney King riots, and various news stories connected with the huge incident. I was aware of the case and like the Floyd incident of 2020 (and many other videos), the video was clear from my standpoint that horrible injustice had taken place via the police. But strangely, up until this time and even in thought of the things I experienced in my upbringing that situation was there, in Los Angeles, and not here for me in Indianapolis.

The brutality of Rodney King was much like that of similar current police violence incidents from Trayvon Martin forward. Not only was his assault by cop horrifying, so too were the reactions that came about after the police who were involved in this beating were acquitted. Short of the viral media and video of the Floyd era and others that smartphones and cop cams have displayed in modern times, for its time, the video of the incident and aftermath was historical and vivid.

When I saw the footage of the Rodney King riots somehow, it was like a time warp of sorts that had me reviewing incidents in my past and present and bringing various circumstances I witnessed or experienced into light in a single moment and thought. That being, yes, race and racism and its ugly residuals are horrifying, repulsive, and long-lasting. More so in this momentous moment, I saw a disadvantaged community, my community, with a trauma so deep, so disenfranchised that its best way to get needed legal or civil rights attention or a respect as humans was to riot in the streets.

While outside that office lounge, I grew up in smaller but similar conditions in the sixteenth largest city in the US, Indianapolis. This was a "light bulb" moment, seeing a different level of collective injustice and unrest. I would like to say that I got up from that break lounge and began to write this book or advocate at many levels to make a difference in my community and country, but it wasn't that like that initially. It was a segment in time that I experienced secondary trauma (some might argue firsthand trauma), if you will, that became a piece of many little pieces that began to radically shape my racial identity and how I was to react to a world I knew existed but up until that time, everything while difficult was normalized, just part of life and you just learned to live with it. It was the first time with maturity, I was stunned at racism and race on a large systematic scale, and truthfully, I couldn't move figuratively because the work of my racial identity and its practical output was in psychological surgery. On the heels of this original Black Lives Matter via the Rodney King dilemma, my transformation with the vast considerations of race began to shape this dialogue. That moment opened the door to unpacking the story that is found in this book.

As an African American male, a kid who grew up in at-risk conditions in an American major city, and now as an adult, a former police officer, current practitioner in the criminal justice system, and a citizen who has experienced enough police stops via profiling, I understand and align with the original focus of Black Lives Matter (BLM); it's as simple as it reads, BLACK-LIVES-MATTER and those lives shouldn't be senselessly killed by law enforcement. I also understand the concept of what was its reactionary, true but misplaced counterpart, Blue Lives Matter. As an American who loves America, I also understand why one would counteract as well with the suggestion of All Lives Matter. Yet again, in my opinion, it is seriously misplaced. Such counteractions to BLM fall very short of this issue at hand historically and contemporarily. This is sticky within American culture, but true to this book and understanding this amazing moment post–George Floyd, there is no question how the heavy hand of the government via policing has been used to hold up racism or has been a consistent vehicle of racism. For a movement to arise in modern America called "Black Lives Matter," shows that the ugly vestiges of our past still live, and certainly, there must be a change in policing and racial implications that surround this issue.

That said, BLM, while necessary and additionally, all movements that focus on the frontline issues of racism, by themselves fall short of what is needed in America in regard to bigger issues at root, not only police violence but also a collection of issues that flow within the criminal justice system. And as America seemingly begins to amend some of the tragedies of this historic era, it will be charged to go deeper to change the plight of disparities within the criminal justice system, a larger overarching theme that is impacting policing and criminal justice reform.

As a mitigation specialist, social worker, and advocate for behavioral change that holistically and truly supports public safety and lowering recidivism, the questions that come to my mind along these lines are continually "what next," "if we stop bad policing, and a racist criminal justice system, what do we do about long-lasting collateral effects or as mentioned collateral consequences," "what do you do about behavior" or "what do we do about an identification and normalization of the criminal justice matters embedded in black and brown lives"? These questions definitely might steer up controversy when unpacked, but the roots of such are valid, at least in this discussion, and I truly believe if we are to truly move beyond the issues of disparities in the criminal justice system, policing, and criminal justice reform, we must grapple with these types of tough questions.

In a quest to understand these types of questions and the thoughts of this book, I have researched various writers and scholarly journals. A book came out in the last decade that was intriguing to me but proved to be very controversial, and frankly, it infuriated me with its false conclusions while resonating and ruminating on the subject matter of going deeper within the criminal justice system. The book was called *Triple Package: How Three Unlikely Traits Explain the Rise and Fall of Cultural Groups in America*, written by Amy Chue and Jed Rudenfeld. It was a motivational book, or at least as the authors described it. Basically, its premise was some American cultural groups outperform other cultures and those cultures that are successful in America embody certain cultural characteristics. According to this book, those characteristics are a superiority complex, impulse control, and then a sense of insecurity. The goal was to motivate its readers to these traits if they wanted to achieve success within their lives or within their cultures.

The natural question might be, "If the book infuriated you, why did you read it?" Well, what was initially attractive about the book for me was that it presented what I'll call a simple sociological addition equation. In this case, it appeared sociologically or psychologically backward. For instance, instead of saying 2 + 2= 4 is an option to reach the quantifiable number of 4, the book suggested an answer of the "4" but did not verify quality answers as to how it arrived at 4. Its conclusions were solely that a 4 existed and made up illegitimate ways it arrived at 4. Moreover, leaving out the fact that while the answer might be 4, there are various ways to get to 4. The "4," in this case, was the book's presupposition that contemporary successful American cultures are successful because of certain factors. In effect and more controversial, cultures that are not successful are deficient in these certain factors. Almost or faintly tickling the edge of alluding to deficient subcultures in America, yes, some minority American cultures.

On the surface, their "4" was what attracted many to the book because in many ways and in a contemporary since it pointed to obvious societal issues. Statistically, some cultures in America are currently more "successful" than others, and if you want to be successful, according to their premise, you must develop and integrate certain aspects in your life and culture for success, thus becoming and being advertised as more of a self-help book. But while I disagree with their conclusions or how they get to the "4" and certainly their suggestions of a deficiency in some cultures that don't have the "4," there is no doubt if any historian or sociologist and even the average person on the street was to look at the current plight of some minority cultures one would have to conclude something is wrong here or perhaps better, something went wrong for these cultures to continue to deal with similar cultural and societal challenges. The book does a nice job of exploring culture to culture, stereotypes, facts, and assumptions, touching on the "elephant in the room" discussions, and then examining the dynamics of certain cultures. I disagreed with most of its conclusions, but I like the discussion. It was bold enough to wrestle with, knowing that it is something many folks might discuss in their safe kitchen tables, work offices, water coolers, and conversational corners. Or in our era of not appearing to be politically incorrect or not being "woke," it's one of those things people might think but don't say: why does said culture seemingly succeed and another said culture historically not succeed as well?

Totally disagreeing with this book's conclusion on why some cultures are less successful in America than others, I invoke the controversial question they suggest in this dialogue to get to a greater point in this book, seemingly, why are some cultures statistically more successful than other cultures? More specific to this discussion, why have we seen all these incidents that brought the rise of Black Lives Matter, the Obama Criminal Justice Reform Legacy, the First Step Act, the George Floyd Act, and the "Change" Movement? Bad policing is obvious, and that obviously needs to change point-blank—end of discussion. While policing is changing and needs to be fixed in America along the lines of criminal justice reform, is there something else we can add to this time of change? With the police violence that occurred with 1992's Rodney King, what more can we learn that still produced the 2020's George Floyd and beyond? Why are there still rampant disparity problems in criminal justice still? While we've seen crime reduce in many areas, why do we still see the sad disparities in the American criminal justice system?

This idea can be seen in the rhetoric of the beleaguered and disgraced but once highly touted "Mayor of America" and tough-on-crime savior of New York City, Mayor Rudy Giuliani of the 2000s. In a 2014 NBC-Meet the Press debate about the Ferguson police officer Darren Wilson in his killing of unarmed teenager Michael Brown, Giuliani was bold about his thoughts on police violence being the black community's fault while debating infamous scholars and authorities on the issues of this book, Dr. Eric Dyson of Vanderbilt University. A consistent thought of Giuliani's during this segmented debate was that he suggested that if the black neighborhoods were not bad, police would not have to be in these neighborhoods, and thus, police violence wouldn't happen. While eloquently refuted by Dr. Dyson and putting forward a false equivalency, Giuliani further noted in this discussion the percentage that "93 percent of blacks are killed by other blacks."[24] This is a key unfortunate example of where the logic of the *Triple Package* books ideology comes to life in policing and criminal justice reform.

As it relates to Black Lives Matter, the Obama Criminal Justice Reform Legacy, the First Step Act, the George Floyd Act, and the "Change" Movement, these types of movements and policies need to continue. But as it relates to the core issues that bring about these movements and policies, there must be a deeper look at ourselves as an American culture to change the diabolical issues we still face on a deeper level and how that sometimes contributes to the very things we often fight against. I need to stress that this is not to abdicate the foundational role of civil rights, activism, policy change, affirmative action, legislation, and needed movements. However, it is to say there is another piece to this puzzle if we want to see full success, especially the major role it has played historically in American jails, prisons, and probation caseloads. While the conclusion of Giuliani and a *Triple Package* isn't remotely correct, we need to grapple with the question of why these issues continue in African American and other minority communities and then what we do about it. Assuredly, racism comes to mind, but racism is not all housed in the issues of policing alone. The greater criminal justice system is problematic, historically racist as well, and has done heavy damage to at-risk minority cultures. Police departments are only one part (albeit very significant) of the "need for change" equation.

While there are various ways to describe what I'm saying, comedy has a major place in my culture to deal with life and serious things and excuse me as I use this medium to further facilitate where I'm going. One of the best places that I've seen this idea of a deeper look at these tough issues expressed in a way that many sides can appreciate is through the comedy of Chris Rock in his heyday.

In my opinion, Rock, in his own right and in many ways was a forerunner of the style that Chappelle became famous for, not only using the same style in his stand-up comedy but on his former HBO show, *The Chris Rock Show*. He, like Chappelle, wasn't afraid to "keep it 100" both inside and outside of the African American culture and was very open to calling out controversy in comedy. On this show, Rock had an infamous sketch that is now repeated over and over again on YouTube. It is a four-minute comedy bit that will have you aghast with laughter, well maybe. In this small snippet of comedic genius, Rock touches on the other side of the issue of BLM, albeit before the rise of the particular movement and within the historical and continued issue of police violence. And dare I go there, absolutely...watch out. Here it comes. If one takes a step back and understands the serious themes of this sketch, it in itself will point to another side of the issue of policing and criminal justice reform while not ignoring the obvious overt issue that police violence needs to stop.

Bluntly and PG-18-rated (my way of meaning some words going forward might be offensive in relation to this example but yet apropos), the Rock sketch is called, *"How not to get your ass kicked by the police!"*[25] The sketch is hilarious as it attempts to not only make fun of horrible policing but also the horrible behaviors that can awake bad policing to its purpose. The sketch is set up with various police car stop scenarios with Rock explaining in a work training video fashion or public service announcement video motif how to not encounter bad police in a negative way. Comedically, he notes the following advice by humorously exemplifying each advice piece in its own skit:

1. Obey the law.
2. Use common sense.
3. Stop immediately.
4. Turn that shit off.
5. Be polite.
6. Shut the fuck up.
7. Get a white friend (to drive).
8. And don't ride with a mad woman.

As you can probably imagine, if you are used to Rock's or Chappelle's comedy, this is crazy hilarious in real time—well, maybe. Both Rock and Chappelle not only shed a deeper light on these types of topics but many others as they relate to race and cultural issues in the United States. This video speaks for itself and can hardly be put into the written word without seeing it for oneself. In a deeper context, it raises the previous questions proposed about BLM, other movements, criminal justice policies, and unrest in our urban cities. What do you do about behavior, or more broadly, a normalization with a crime or the criminal justice system embedded in the African American and minority American experience? Let me add in the other hidden controversial questions highlighted by referencing the book, *The Triple Package*.

Before you drop or burn this book, try to look deeper. Allow me again to reiterate, from this professional's standpoint, I will attest again, again, and again, that the policing issues we have seen most recently and historically embedded in American culture need to be addressed unequivocally, swiftly, and forthrightly and shouldn't be an issue in modern-day America. Policing has to change; black lives really do matter. Also, the recently passed and current criminal justice policies and their evolution need to continue. No civilized society can truly walk forward in civility and humanity, allowing unlawful police practices to continue. Additionally, the cause of civil rights and the criminal justice system need to continue because racism is alive, systematic, and, as I noted, entrenched in what I think to be the last leg of expansive and systematic racism: the criminal justice system. However, there is another side that exists that gets little attention. It goes deeper than horrible policing and overt racism. It goes far deeper than the incubator of poverty and life in our urban cities or the latest inner-city problem that is glamorized in the news. Yes, it goes deeper than the absolutely horrible cops with racist tendencies and trigger-happy fingers.

Beyond my failed comedic attempt to highlight this thought (working on my comedy tour) and further my use of the controversial book *The Triple Package*, Dr. Martin Luther King Jr. hits the target of where I'm going perfectly in his 1967 speech, "What Is Your Life's Blueprint." Six months before his tragic assassination, Dr. King spoke as he so giftedly did on many historic occasions, this time to a group of students at Barratt Junior High School in Philadelphia. There's no better way to understand and appreciate the power and depth of it than listening to the speech. However, citing some of its words fit so well here:

> This is the most important and crucial period of your lives. For what you do now and what you decide now at this age may well determine which way your life shall go. And whenever a building is constructed, you usually have an architect who draws a blueprint. And that

blueprint serves as the pattern, as the guide, as the model, for those who are to build the building. And a building is not well erected without a good, sound, and solid blueprint. Now each of you is in the process of building the structure of your lives, and the question is: whether you have a proper, a solid, and a sound blueprint.

Number one in your life's blueprint should be: a deep belief in your own dignity, your own worth and your own somebodiness. Don't allow anybody to make you feel that you are nobody. Always feel that you count. Always feel that you have worth, and always feel that your life has ultimate significance.

Secondly, in your life's blueprint, you must have as a basic principle the determination to achieve excellence in your various fields of endeavor. You're going to be deciding as the days and the years unfold what you will do in life, what your life's work will be. Once you discover what it will be, set out to do it and to do it well. Be a bush if you can't be a tree. If you can't be a highway, just be a trail. If you can't be the sun, be a star, for it isn't by size that you win or you fail, be the best of whatever you are.

And finally, in your life's blueprint must be a commitment to the eternal principles of beauty, love, and justice. Don't allow anybody to pull you so low as to make you hate them. Don't allow anybody to cause you to lose your self-respect to the point that you do not struggle for justice. However young you are, you have a responsibility to seek to make your nation a better nation in which to live.[26]

Within this eloquent speech, Dr. King talks about having a "blueprint," he speaks about knowing one's "own worth," and he pinpoints the necessity of knowing one's "somebodiness." All are synonymous with knowing the essence of one's identity. This speech speaks forward and says fight the fight, push for criminal justice reform, march for change, and shout "Black Lives Matter," but in all that doing, know your blueprint, know the essence of your amazing identity even amid the challenge of racism, police violence, and its various outgrowths.

As noted earlier, if we stopped the behavior of bad cops and enacted all the various front-end policies, it would still leave many with the ravages of historical trauma where criminality has become normality, and the criminal justice system would still be overwhelmed with disparities of black and brown lives. If the goal is to stop not only the bad policing but also criminal justice reform, if the goal is lowering disparities of African Americans in the criminal legal system at some point and not to any cessation of civil rights and policy change on the front-end of these issues, at some point, the movement must turn or dramatically expand its concentration to internal transformation, Dr. King's "somebodiness" and his call for a proper "blueprint".

Then practically upon that galvanizing policies, corrective processes and treatment/behavioral change structures around the contemplation of how to change the collective historical trauma, normalization of crime, and cultural collateral consequences of historic incarceration on individual personal and cultural identities. This bigger focus would not only tackle policing but courts, jails, prisons, probation, and corrections and specifically how they deal with the lives already impacted by incarceration and the lives that still will be impacted by the legal system. This idea goes toward a deeper idea of criminal justice reform.

Black Lives Do Matter, but they matter as well to the at-risk young man and young lady who lost their parents to historic incarceration. Black Lives Do Matter, but they matter as well to that young man who has been in prison for twenty years and has no ability to acclimate in a beneficial way to a prosocial life after prison.

Black Lives Do Matter, but they matter as well to that young lady who thinks education isn't attainable or not associated with positive characteristics of her culture. Black Lives Do Matter, but they matter as well to the scores of young people who think a two-parent home was only a fictitious, fake, and now historical display on the iconic comedy, *The Cosby Show*. Black Lives Do matter, but it matters as well to those systems of professionals in place to change the culture of policing and criminal justice reform but have no African Americans or minorities in places of leadership to give a context to a real change. Black Lives Do Matter, but it matters in prisons and jails that don't have access to quality higher education, vocational education, chemical dependency and mental health care. Black Lives Do Matter, but it matters beyond that young youth that thinks entertainment or sports are the only way out or up for an African American. Black Lives Do Matter, but it matters to the urban schools that don't have quality education and continually become a part of the Pipeline to Prison and highlight what is the Achievement Gap. Indeed, Black Lives Matter, but for holistic change, the movement must go deeper and be supported as such via policy within state and federal offices.

As mentioned earlier, I read the book *The Triple Package*. Among other books I read were two that had similar controversial conclusions and titles for that matter. But their conclusions were not sensational or meant to stir controversy. They had significant research to back their conclusions. Get ready. The titles are total "keep it real," and some would note controversial as well, but they are applicable in grappling with the concerns noted here. Here are the titles: *Marriage Is for White People* (Ralph Richard Banks, 2011), and then the other book is *Multiplication Is for White People* (Lisa Delpit, 2012). Given their hard statistics, their conclusions as to the lack of strength of traditional marriage in African American culture and the academic challenges within African American culture were solid but mentioned the impact of racism and the need for internal change. These books not only noted the facts and the problems, but they also noted the aperture of a positive identity with traditional marriage and education, this being a principal problem as to why these areas exhibit a lack of consistent health within at-risk African American communities. They concluded that if one agrees there is a problem with marriage in the black culture and if there is a problem with education being a high priority within African American cultures, it is because there isn't a positive identity in these areas. Going back to Dr. King, these areas are not a hallmark of the needed life blueprint.

These books and the issues they champion can be debated, but their practicality is real as one born out of due time, having experienced these issues personally and seeing these matters play out in the day to day in my career. Black Lives Matter, the Obama Criminal Justice Reform Legacy, the First Step Act, the George Floyd Act, and the "Change" Movement are dynamics that point to a strong and needed effort of continual change. However, if there is not an attempt to recalibrate a sense of positive identity amongst at-risk African Americans in the criminal justice system and after decades and decades of oppressive racism via policing, the criminal justice system, and its very sad collateral consequences, these efforts will not reach its intended goals. Indeed, policing practices need to change, and movements are afoot, and thankfully, the tide is slowly changing via recent convictions on bad policing, such as the conviction of police officer Derek Chauvin. But the energy and the action toward change cannot stop there because these movements and policies are symbols of what has occurred historically and with cultural collateral impacts. There's work to do within justice systems and corrections to build back up the somebodiness of those disproportionately stuck in jails and prisons.

CHAPTER 4

In the Trenches A Public Defender and Social Work Perspective

As a public defender, mitigation specialist, and social worker, I sat energetically on the witness stand in a county court, testifying on behalf of a talented African American youth who was facing sentencing for various charges. As I sat there eager to testify, I thought that my testimony, riddled with philosophical suggestions for the court, would not only lead to my recommendation for an alternative disposition other than a punitive juvenile correctional placement for our client. But also, and audacious on my part, I also thought that my hard work, research, and preparation would ignite a cultural evolution within the criminal justice system; a revolution that pushed for a holistic view of disparities with at-risk minority youth in the criminal justice system and towards creative, cultural, and competent solutions for the many minorities that frequent jails and prisons.

As the assistant public defender or our defense attorney began to extract my testimony to support our alternative idea to the court, it seemed she strategically had few questions, and the ones that were asked were open-ended, to allow me the ability to indirectly argue for a disposition without a need for continuous questioning from her. I seized the opportunity and, as I thought, presented to the court a valuable landscape of dispositional expertise and acute options for our client's correctional needs, treatment-oriented needs and, of course, in support of public safety. The judge not only considered my dispositional alternative thoughts but also my lofty ideals, inquiring himself to me directly about what I was espousing.

After my testimony, both the prosecution and our defense had their closing arguments for sentencing. Both arguments were great, but it was clear that our defense argument was much more applicable and advantageous, challenging the judge to rule in our client's favor. Consistent with the judge's style, he was slow and methodical as he began to make his decision. A white-headed and experienced judge, almost Senator Bernie Sanders-eske in appearance, at his bench quiet with his head down, flipping through the case file and rubbing his forehead as he made his decision. The case concluded, and the court ruled in favor of the prosecution primarily due to the fact there were no local treatment or corrective options that matched my recommendation. Young in public defender work at the time, I felt frustrated and a little puzzled.

The combination of feelings was all the more stirred when the distinguished and exemplary judge said to me, "Mr. Bailey, when you find the solutions for the court that you are describing, I will consider those solutions as it relates to disparities within the criminal justice system."

As an advocate of the public defender, it is important to bring in the value of this work and its holistic application and championing of the issues of disparities in the criminal justice system. This work extends via the basis of the United States Supreme Court in Gideon v. Wainright when it recognized that the fundamental right to a fair trial requires an indigent person accused of a crime to have the assistance of competent counsel. As the constitutional champions of *equal protection under the law* this work is dedicated to protecting society's most powerless people and assisting the American ideal where everyone's constitutional rights are upheld. Moreover, as a social worker in the public defender field, my work consists of finding the deeper issues as they relate to clientele in the criminal justice system and then communicating those thoughts as they relate to proper sentencing and outcomes in criminal court. This involves research, community advocacy, many one-on-one meetings, collaboration with various criminal justice and mental health professionals, and assessments of our clientele, not to mention a myriad of other aspects to support the work advocating for clients from a criminal defense and public defender standpoint.

As the thoughts from this book and toward the criminal justice system develop, it is important to note that this perspective comes from a public defender and social work perspective and a practitioner of this work. I acknowledge there are tremendous disciplines and experts that speak to these issues, from criminologists to mental health professionals, sociologists, scientists, educators, nonprofit organizations, spiritual professionals, think tanks, and policy-oriented entities. There are many who competently and authoritatively speak to this issue of disparities in the criminal justice system and what is best to do about it. Some of these are what I have used to support and develop this frame of mind. However, to truthfully consider the focus of this book and what I contend is a current missing link to the issue of minorities historically overriding jails, prisons, and probation caseloads, the perspective or philosophy from the level of the social work profession in the public defender field provide a great context to think differently about the previous and forward matters discussed.

In reference to this perspective, it is good to understand the context of this book from the idea of approaching the vast issues of the disparities in the criminal justice system from a strength-based approach. Dennis Salebeey on social work practice provides context with these thoughts he develops:

- All individuals in our communities have strengths.
- Adversity can be a positive force while still being challenging.
- It is the job of this work to understand the personal or communal motivations and aspirations for behavior change and use those for augmenting change.
- The support process must be collaborative between the client and the change agent to support true change.
- And strengths can be found in any environment. Personal change is indigenous.[27]

In total, it's my job to, directly and indirectly, discover the deeper aspects at play with those that are in the criminal justice system in an effort to direct the court to seek the best appropriate sentences, to rely on alternative methods other than prison, and more appropriate sentencing to prison that speak to meeting the public safety and punitive concerns while paying close attention to recidivism, effectively what will keep offenders from never coming back into the criminal justice system. This means focusing on the strengths of the client and also strengths that will uphold the community in relationship to the client. The primary focus then becomes what is best for public safety, behavioral change, and lowered recidivism. This is the arena this book comes from and where it is going.

As I do my work traveling from courthouse to courthouse and jail to jail and in the various places I've worked in this capacity (spanning from Minnesota, Arizona, and Colorado), I see upfront the disparity statistics and realities previously described. I also see the greater context that policing and incarceration revolve around daily and in various aspects. As a trainer who has been privileged to train along this subject matter throughout America, I've been able to brainstorm and rub shoulders with amazing minds and practitioners in this field who grapple with this same subject matter. Also, as a student of this work and learning more and more about this subject matter, I often muse and ponder about this and what are necessary outcomes. Collectively and conclusively, it is very apparent to me that the criminal justice system and corrective and treatment measures have been slow or indifferent to develop or display competencies, standards, and staffing patterns to adequately deal with the issue of multi-cultural overcrowding jails and prisons.

This is said in the face of the growth of evidence-based practices (EBP) in many areas, such as chemical dependency, mental health focus, and the advancement of numerous correctional and treatment-oriented practices and modalities in criminal justice. This is said with the advancement of quality measurement tools to assist criminal justice and correctional outcomes, such as the *level of service/case management inventory* (LS/CMI). The field is littered with assessment tool after assessment tool, study after study, research after research, conference after conference, new treatment practice after practice, new phraseology/theories, and the latest, not to mention the innumerable high-level professionals working in the correctional, treatment, research and policy fields all over America. With all of these and more yet again, as I see day after day, the disparity totals previously mentioned continued year after year.

Professionally, I have sat on committee after committee and board after board and heard of the many advances and buzzwords that have led to or will lead to a reduction in crime. None of them have come up with a bona fide solution to the answer as to why a group that is around 13 percent of the United States population is close to 40 percent of the United States prison population, the African American culture. As stated before, a racist justice system or a system with residuals of historic racism has been suggested and proved to be the main culprit. Conceding to that reality, and while efforts continue and need to continue to change, no recent professional criminal justice endeavors have come up with viable, practical answers to change the plight of young African American men continuing to recidivate back into prisons.

General practices and research can speak to this and conclude from their diverse points on criminal justice disproportionality. But no programming or research dares to "go there" with cultural specificity within the criminal justice arena, especially within the corrections departments all across America. While much has improved in cultural competency in various areas, from social workers and police forces in law enforcement, and again, the various improvements sought by various presidential offices, the criminal justice system is still struggling with adopting a holistic and better response to crime and punishment and multicultural jails and prisons. The historic racist piece is obvious, the disparity statistics are obvious, this historic intentionality and cultural collateral consequences are obvious, the need to fight for the civil rights of old within the criminal justice system is obvious, efforts toward this fight have been obvious, yet change is not obvious.

It must be said that social service focus, treatment philosophies, and counseling efforts, such as the National Counseling Association (NCA), have created modalities on this issue with implemented agendas to work on this idea of a cultural identity crisis and its enculturation of negative behaviors. This will be further developed later, but encouragingly, there is much movement and training toward these efforts in the social service, treatment, and counseling arena.

A simple example of this trend is found in the book *Bridges to Recovery: Addiction, Family Therapy, and Multicultural Treatment.* In their piece on CD treatment for the Native American population, they espouse the following:

> The urgent need for large-scale sobriety among Indian people calls for a more culturally specific model. The Indian sobriety movement uses various approaches to sobriety. One of the common threads is pride: pride in tradition, pride in culture, and pride in being an Indian. Using one's culture adjunct to recovery provides an ally which unlocks emotional energy in the service of sobriety.[28]

This excerpt captures impeccably the essence of identity and its place in treatment. It underscores its need for the best treatment outcomes. However, while social service and counseling disciplines have realized a need to focus on identity and culture, the criminal justice system has been slow in adopting this focus.

Nationwide trends point to the fact that the criminal justice system is measured in its practical response to the idea of treatment or corrective modalities influenced by one's cultural norms or identity or even the idea of a multi-cultural corrections practice. There are research and frameworks for implementation to assist with dealing with disparities in criminal justice. As example is Sam Houston State University's Dr. Robert A. Shearer and Dr. Patricia Ann King, in their article *Multicultural Competencies in Probation—Issues and Challenges*, use a similar word "worldview" to describe this cultural idea and further lay a panoramic context for the motif of this report, addressing therapeutically this "worldview" or cultural identity crisis,

> Chung and Bernak (2002) maintain that helpers must develop cultural empathy, which

> they view as the ability to demonstrate and communicate an understanding of the client's worldview. Basically, a worldview is the ways in which individuals perceive their relationship to the world as shaped through their culture. It is therefore essential that helpers communicate an understanding of the client's worldview. There are six steps that can be taken to demonstrate cultural empathy. First, the counselor must understand and accept the context of family and community for clients from different cultural backgrounds. Second, counselors should incorporate indigenous healing practices from the client's culture whenever possible. Third, counselors must become knowledgeable about the historical and sociopolitical background of clients. Fourth, they must become knowledgeable of the psychosocial adjustment that must be made by clients who have moved from one environment to another. Fifth, they must be sensitive to the oppression, discrimination, and racism encountered by many people. Finally, counselors must facilitate empowerment for those clients who feel underprivileged and devalued.[29]

This, in a nutshell, is an idea of a proactive action toward disparities. However, implementation is a problem, as previously mentioned.

While this does not get as much attention when it comes to crime, punishment, race, and disparities, it is very important. It is the idea of cultural competence in the work of the criminal justice system and using it as a main backdrop to assist with lowering criminal justice disparities.

In explanation or as an example, what comes to mind are the lyrics from the old rap song "Gangsta's Paradise," a classic for those who love the golden era of hip-hop. This song was seemingly the theme song of another classic of its time and related to the powerful time for this book's premise (1994 that ushed in the higher and historical level of mass incarceration[30]), the 1995 infamous inner-city school movie *Dangerous Minds*. This movie focuses on the lives of urban Latino and African American students and the efforts of an ambitious teacher to pull them out of crime and violence. This song won the 1996 Grammy Award for Best Rap Solo Performance by then-famous rapper Coolio. Various lyrics within the song speak to the cries of a life of crime, poverty, and historical trauma. Such phrases as:

> Look at the situation they got me facing
> I can't live a normal life, I was raised by the street
> So I gotta be down with the hood team
> Too much television watchin', got me chasing dreams

Or the phrase,

> Fool, death ain't nothin' but a heart beat away
> I'm livin' life do or die, what can I say?
> I'm 23 now but will I live to see 24?
> The way things is going I don't know"

At one point, the famous rap song speaks toward a hope-deferred in one phrase, "They say I've got to learn, but nobody's here to teach me. If they can't understand it, how can they reach me." In context with this movie, song, and extremely consequent policy era for mass incarceration, it points toward and demands an acclimation of the human service or criminal justice practitioner or policy maker to understand, relate to, and operate in conjunction with the cultural needs of the client. Hip-hop music, as easily known, is the language of the at-risk African American, among other aspects of the African American culture. Time does not permit the display of the various words on the street that cry against racism, police violence, conditions of the inner-city, and even black identity. I'm an old schooler, as said by my oldest daughter who has sought to update me on current hip-hop and its voice of the streets and people. I need to stay in my lane here. But suffice it to say rap music is a musical panorama of the thought of this book

In a totally different mindset, consider an analogy from the business world with regard to this growing focus. If a clientele base of a certain business was 40 percent of its total revenue base, that business would most assuredly cater to that clientele base in various cultural-specific efforts from advertisements, product selection, and staffing patterns to win and keep that 40 percent, a main part of the company's bottom line. Now this mindset is somewhat off and averse, and I apologize as I'm adopting two totally different disciplines. But consider America's criminal justice system given the high totals of minority Americans in its systems and continually so, why then is it not culturally competent to cater to the needs of its clientele? A larger question that will not be tackled in this book but gives strength to the premise is why isn't the criminal justice system, lawyer, cop, correctional officer, judge, policy maker, and counselor, administration and staffing patterns not even close as diverse as the clientele it serves? Certainly, minorities aren't a business constituency of the criminal justice system (well, depending on if you believe some conspiracy theories), but it is a main part of its clientele; then with the goals of said "rehabilitation" and "corrections," even "evidence-based practices," should it at least be mandatorily culturally competent in its law enforcement, court, corrective, and therapeutic processes; not to mention its staffing and leadership patterns?

Respectful to the business field and its obvious differences from the criminal justice discipline, think again about the continued disparities in jails and prisons. Why does it continue? Why is it still an issue in the 2020s and beyond? As I work day-in and day-out with these clientele, I see the high amounts of minorities in the system and the various issues that come along with these populations. Respectfully, there is much movement, research, attempts, and posturing toward the issue of disparities within criminal justice work. The whole notion of criminal justice reform has as its foundation, changing the plight of disparities in jails and prisons. I have researched and been a part of studies and programs that speak to these issues. As I briefly presented, there are conclusions or thoughts as to cultural competence in regard to these issues. Motion is afoot, but the criminal justice system is sadly falling short in my professional view, and per the statistics related to disparities, it is obviously not changing.

In an effort to find lasting change, criminal justice reform, and discontinue its historical relationship with disparities, there must be a larger focus and willingness to go deeper if it wants to solve this problem. Mass incarceration and its disparity issues cannot continue if criminal justice reform is to happen. With true change in mind, I ask the difficult question, the elephant in the room question, "why is mass incarceration specific to minority groups historically and contemporarily still so prevalent? In my research and just working in criminal justice, I've heard various answers, debates, and deliberations that have grappled with these types of questions and the possible root of this quandary: some valid, some not so valid, and some just absolutely crazy. Those would involve secondary questions similar to the following,

- is it just a propensity crime that naturally exists for the community of these populations,
- is it a racist criminal justice system,
- is it racist law enforcement practices,
- is it racist and ignorant policies, such as the 1994 Crime Bill,
- is it the culture of poverty,
- is it dysfunctional family structures,
- is it just choices,
- is it a spiritual issue,
- is it a lack of education,
- Is it mental health?

While these questions and others are discussed and researched, and while I understand the many potential foundational aspects to criminal behavior proven through research, and while these and other aspects have valid foundations to debate why disparities exist,

I professionally attest to another foundational aspect that does not receive much practical attention, and I believe it is a key component to competently assist with changing the last truly powerful bastion of systemic racism in America, the criminal justice system. Going back to something I've been referring to, that other aspect is that there is a cultural identity crisis with most at-risk minorities from historically oppressed cultures after centuries of the collateral consequences of incarceration of a culture. Moreover, and as a solution to the previous "elephant in the room" question, treatment and corrective modalities within criminal justice, jails, prisons, courts, and probation caseloads need to focus on this idea of a cultural identity crisis to assist with changing the high totals of minorities in the criminal justice system. Merely, the front-end push, as I call it, while imperatively needed, is not enough. There must be a policy-led and backed movement across the United States to work on this cultural identity crisis for true change with this continual disparity issue within the criminal justice system.

CHAPTER 5

A Theory for Practical Change Rumination

"Nick" (not the actual name), and African American youth, was another amazing athlete I had the pleasure of working with. As a youth, he showed an impressive aptitude for sports. It was his passion, his fun, and his outlet. Coupled with his athletic skills was his personable nature and comfortable, cool vibe that made him a stranger to no one.

Unfortunately, Nick came from a notorious criminal family, and social service and correctional interventions in his life started early to hopefully curb him following in the footsteps of his family members. He, unlike many, found a haven in the local social service system and was in and out of the foster care system as a young kid, which eventually guided him through the rough patches of the criminality and aberrant lifestyle that was so akin to his family while he made it through his grade school years well. High school initially became a promising opportunity for Nick. With his sports prowess and positive support in his life, things continued to manage well.

As he got closer to his senior year, he began to struggle with his behaviors and tempting his criminal roots. However, he maintained an upward trajectory toward finishing school and playing sports in college. While this was going on, many within his family challenged him toward criminality, a life far different than the promising life and behavior he was building for himself. Pretty soon, Nick was consumed by his family's ties to criminality, and he too was facing a prison sentence. As I worked with him, I heard something that keyed my interest in why he began to fall from the life he was making for himself. Apparently, a member of his family said in so many words that Nick was not good at the family trade, crime, and drug dealing culture. When I heard this, it quickly appeared to me that he was struggling with his identity and the pressure and familiarity with criminality as opposed to living positively. It also appeared that it was tough that his family wasn't supportive of his positive endeavors.

To look at the life of Nick is to look at the life of many at-risk minority young men and women I've worked with in my history in this work, and I'd dare say many at-risk minorities throughout the United States. For those who work with at-risk youth or young adults in social services, corrections, nonprofits, treatment programs, courts, or the law enforcement business, you have worked with these types of scenarios. You can reproduce this story repeatedly. They range from sad to very tragic. Not all are sports prodigies. In fact, few are. It could be that promising young lady with academic talent, that young father who so desperately wants to be a great dad to his kids, that kid with an amazing aptitude for auto mechanics, a youth with a talent and passion for the arts, or even those youth and young adults with commendable aspirations to make a difference in their communities by aspiring careers as lawyers, doctors, nurses, and teachers. There could be many angles or ideas with which many would conclude as to why these young men or young women, when given proper support, mixed with talent and opportunity, often go back to the challenging people and conditions they were born in. The conclusions are bountiful, and the overall criminal justice system needs to be open to the various reasons as to why.

As I worked with Nick and witnessed his impressive ability to separate himself from the criminality so familiar to his family and upbringing, the negative identity of his family's criminality inundated him so severely and had tugged at him so much that he succumbed to that lifestyle, its familiarity, and yes, even its comfort. A review of his life would reveal various aspects of concern as to why he became an eventual slave to his family's criminality. Having known Nick for a good part of his life, it was very apparent to me, given all the anchors he had and struggles he had to work through, that nothing was more momentous than the struggle for what he was to identify with as who he was and what his future was to be. In my professional opinion and amid the myriads of therapeutic, psychological, sociological, societal, economic, and cognitive perspectives that could conclude differently on this and other similar scenarios, while Nick began to adopt a different way of life and future for himself the identity of his family won in the most critical time in which he could escape the horrible problems that plagued his family. Nick eventually went to prison as an adult and struggled in and out of the criminal justice system. As well, the advantages he built for himself were all but choked away because of the overwhelming challenges and weight of crime and its results. Amid his various challenges, I contend a large issue he struggled with is the idea of a cultural identity crisis.

Antoine de Saint-Exupéry, the French writer and aviator, once wrote, "A civilization is a heritage of beliefs, customs, and knowledge slowly accumulated in the course of centuries, elements difficult at times to justify by logic, but justifying themselves as paths when they lead somewhere, since they open up for man his inner distance."[31] In a snapshot, this quote describes the course of this book and this theory of a cultural identity crisis, and more importantly, the central place and core of what identity means and its ability to guide the life course of individuals, cultures, and civilizations. This is the crux of where I will begin to ruminate in depth in hopes of examining how focusing on the idea of a cultural identity crisis and then a strength-based counterpart, positive identity development, can be impactful within the criminal justice system, assist in lowering disparities, and also be a foundation for other disciplines that deal with the residuals of the criminal justice system and the unfortunate disparities and collateral consequences it produces.

As previously noted, I contend that the epidemic with at-risk minorities within the criminal justice system, and amid "best practices," "evidence-based practices," the criminal justice system, in its efforts to correct and rehabilitate, is failing at-risk minorities, sadly failing its largest proportionate populations. As also mentioned, to combat this issue, most activism to change this issue has focused on the fact that the criminal justice system is racist or has racist tendencies, specifically with front-end dynamics. It is clear that the criminal justice system has historical and contemporary problems with racism within its structures, and change with the problems is a vast necessity. However, there is an issue not being ruminated nearly as much, and that issue points to a cultural identity crisis and a consequent culture of clients that identify with criminality as somewhat of normality or a cultural "settling" for the holistic cultural weight of the criminal justice system and that adjacent to the totality of its ramifications.

This notion of a cultural identity crisis is not new, and via its many other similar names, thoughts, and descriptions, it has been thoroughly developed and influenced the philosophy of some practices, among them what we've previously mentioned, social service practice. While not new, the thoughts and ideas around this subject matter are not in a practical daily movement within criminal justice circles as much as it is researched and developed. Whether my specific notion of this cultural identity crisis is debated or challenged (and I thoroughly invite critical thought on this that leads toward a full answer to this quandary and lowering of disparities), diversity and culture are the current criminal justice system. It inundates its jails, prisons, courts, and probation caseloads. Additionally, cultural competence is not a hallmark of the criminal justice system. The Black Lives Matter and front-end policies on the frontend of our advocacy are sadly the same black lives (and other disparities) that matter after incarceration, during incarceration, and after being overwhelmed by the criminal justice system. Easily and an obvious repeat, this is a significant issue that, despite years of effort to address disparities, it is still powerfully evident. Albeit the systems built to change and correct behavior, by and large, have ignored thoughts toward cultural competence in their practices, despite being historically and heavily diverse in their clientele.

This notion or idea of a cultural identity crisis in this context is developed from the sociological basis of at-risk minorities from racially and historically oppressed groups in America. This would include primarily the Native American and the African American cultures due to their high proportionality in the national criminal justice system and its correlation to oppressed minorities. This would also include Latino Americans and their high totals in the criminal justice system as well. Personally, being an African American, my professional strengths are with the African American culture, and given this culture has the highest totals in criminal justice, I will speak mostly from this vantage point. However, I do believe the general concepts can be applicable to other at-risk cultures that are disproportionate in the criminal justice system.

Understanding disparities and overcrowded jails and prisons, filled with the "Nicks" of America, necessitates and understanding of what this is, and why it is proposed is an imperative element in the battle for criminal justice reform. To unpack the theory of a cultural identity crisis and its importance, basic definitions, various facets of minority identity, and practical methodologies focused on identity and its implications in instruction, treatment, and corrections must be considered for context. The following is a brief and non-exhaustive review of foundational concepts that give life to this idea of a cultural identity crisis within the criminal justice system.

Key Definitions

Identity[32]

> —the distinguishing character or personality of an individual: INDIVIDUALITY b: the relation established by psychological identification

Crisis[33]

1. a. the turning point for better or worse in an acute disease or fever
   b. a paroxysmal attack of pain, distress, or disordered function
2. c. an emotionally significant event or radical change of status in a person's life

3. : the decisive moment (as in a literary plot)
   a. an unstable or crucial time or state of affairs in which a decisive change is impending
   b. a situation that has reached a critical phase

Cultural[34]

—of or relating to culture or culturing

Culture[35]

a. the customary beliefs, social forms, and material traits of a racial, religious, or social group *also*: the characteristic features of everyday existence (such as diversions or a way of life) shared by people in a place or time
b. the set of shared attitudes, values, goals, and practices that characterize an institution or organization
c. the set of values, conventions, or social practices associated with a particular field, activity, or societal characteristic
d. the integrated pattern of human knowledge, belief, and behavior that depends upon the capacity for learning and transmitting knowledge to succeeding generations

Identity Crisis
Erik Erickson

Further, we must describe "identity crisis" as coined by foundational psychologist Erik Erikson. According to Erikson, the term identity crisis refers to a social psychological theory in which an individual loses a sense of personal sameness and historical foundation.

Educational Psychologist Kendra Cherry gives a good description of Erickson's term an "identity crisis" and its relation to the concept of a cultural identity crisis. Dr. Cherry describes, "According to Erikson, an identity crisis is a time of intensive analysis and exploration of different ways of looking at oneself."[36] In the review of

Erikson's own personal analysis, we understand that his interest in identity began in childhood.

> Raised Jewish, Erikson appeared very Scandinavian and often felt that he was an outsider of both groups. His later studies of cultural life among the Yurok of northern California and the Sioux of South Dakota helped formalize Erikson's ideas about identity development and identity crisis.[37]

Erickson himself gives a greater and more profound context of an identity crisis when he describes his identity crisis via "psycho" and "social" dynamics:

Psycho:

- It is partially conscious and partially unconscious. It is a sense of personal continuity and sameness, but it is also a quality of unself-conscious living, as can be so gloriously obvious in a young person who has found himself as he has found his communality. In him, we see emerge a unification of what is irreversibly given (that is, body type and temperament, giftedness and vulnerability, infantile models and ingrained prejudices) with the open choices provided (available roles, occupational possibilities, values offered, friendships made, sexual encounters), and all this within traditional or emerging cultural and historical patterns.
- It is beset with the dynamics of conflict, and especially at its climax, it can lead to contradictory mental states such as a sense of aggravated vulnerability and, alternatively, one of grand individual promise.
- It has its own developmental period, before which it could not come to a crisis because the somatic, cognitive, and social preconditions are not yet given, and beyond which, it must not be delayed because the next and all future

developments depend on it. This developmental period is, of course, adolescence and youth, which also means that the identity crisis partially depends on psychobiological factors, which secure the somatic basis for an organism's coherent sense of vital selfhood.

- It reaches both into the past and toward the future: it is grounded in the stages of childhood and will dep.

Social:

- The crisis is sometimes hardly noticeable and sometimes very much so: in some young people, in some classes, at some periods in history, the identity crisis will be noiseless; in other people, classes, and periods, the crisis will be clearly marked off as a critical period, a kind of "second birth," institutionalized by ceremonial procedure, or intensified by collective strife or individual conflict.
- Identity formation normatively has its negative side, which throughout life can remain an unruly part of the total identity. The negative identity is the sum of all those identifications and identity fragments that the individual had to submerge in himself as undesirable or irreconcilable or by which atypical individuals and marked minorities are made to feel "different." In the event of aggravated crises, an individual may despair of the ability to contain these negative elements in a positive identity. A specific rage can be aroused wherever identity development loses the promise of a traditionally assured wholeness; thus, an as-yet uncommitted delinquent may become a criminal.
- The nature of the identity conflict often depends on the latent panic pervading a historical period. Some periods in history become identity vacuums caused by three basic forms of human apprehension: fears aroused by new facts, such as discoveries and inventions (which radically expand and change the whole world-image; anxieties aroused by symbolic dangers vaguely perceived as a consequence of the

> decay of existing ideologies; and the dread of an existential abyss devoid of spiritual meaning.[38]

Of an identity crisis notes as Erikson alludes to, this can impact adulthood. She further notes, "Erikson noted that developing a sense of identity is important during the teenage years, though the formation and growth of identity is not confined to adolescence. Instead, identity shifts and changes throughout life as people confront new challenges and tackle different experiences. Thus, an identity crisis can occur at any age."[39]

All the previous describe the definition and formation of an identity crisis. It also displays common issues that speak to this dynamic. Displayed are race, religion, region, bicultural identity, and then consequent feelings of alienation and uncertainty. In combination with the term "cultural," "cultural identity crisis" in this context refers to when a culture, as defined, is challenged to change and morph its collective identity or identities due to outside pressures such as racism. More specifically, in this context, it occurs when systems (the criminal justice system) and the historic racist structures and the lingering effects of racism play a significant role in one's identity and consequent behavior.

The idea of an identity crisis and its meaning is cyclical and a common topic within African America. In her book *Codes of Conduct: Race, Ethics, and the Color of our Character*, Professor Karla Holloway describes identity crisis in these terms of the familiar matriarchal family system:

> Ironically, the identity of color that mother and legions before her have used to restrict and yoke a black child's conduct is also a collaborative cultural affirmation. As this "also" links negative purpose to redemptive communion, it locates the necessary ambiguity within Codes of Conduct. In one critical sense, racialized discourse enunciates the malicious impact of language that has articulated, legislated and enforced policies and

> processes that have institutionalized themselves by reifying the lie of a biological referent. In this regimented space, race identifies what out of a biologized history of cultural conflict has been rendered true and actual based on a perversion of science.
>
> In the same space, however, there is a tracery of cultural work, including language, belief, artistry, custom and value that have emerged precisely because of the ubiquitous presence of race in public life. The presence and practice of the African American community that practices this cultural work in the United States forces a convergence of memory and history, practice and process that is both racial and ethnic.[40]
>
> In Erik Erikson's stages of psychosocial development, the emergence of an identity crisis occurs during the teenage years in which people struggle between feelings of identity versus role confusion. Erickson's Freudian style of psychosocial theory describes the impact of social experience throughout a person's life. This theory is the supportive theory is the basis of the idea of a cultural identity crisis.

To reaffirm, such thoughts and terminology is not new. Various terms describe the same or similar dynamic. As it relates to this notion of a cultural identity crisis, there are various major themes that help develop this notion: the soul wound, historical trauma, post-traumatic slave syndrome, racial identity development, ethnic-racial identity development, and positive identity development. A review of these terms is merely just scratching the surface of the breath of concepts of study within this realm, but they provide a basis for this focus of our view of the criminal justice system and thoughts toward criminal justice reform. These themes serve as foundational key concepts in understanding at-risk and historically oppressed minorities, groups that overwhelm the American criminal justice system.

Additionally, as I will highlight, there are many scholars with various scientific and well-researched conclusions that would give what I'm describing as a cultural identity crisis different names or phraseology. Moreover, these are the anchors that give this discourse foundation. In my professional opinion, these further should be anchors for modalities that will assist efforts seeking to build philosophical foundations and programmatic outcomes to deal with building a holistic and full criminal justice reform that hits at the issue of actually changing the historic disparity problem. The verbiage and idea of a cultural identity crisis give an understanding of how to address disparities in the criminal justice system more expansively. In my professional opinion, it best describes what I see in the many Nicks within the criminal justice system and further gives light on how to address this issue in a revolutionary way.

CHAPTER 6

Foundational Concepts for Context

Within my public defender career and community outreach by way of that work, I became so convinced of this issue of a cultural identity crisis that I began a program within my local area at the time. I wanted to research this idea to address this issue and also to provide and incubator of research to foster evidence that there is (or isn't) a need for culturally competent programming in all main social, educational, and, specifically, in my case criminal justice entities that work with high minority disparities.

I built the program and curriculum, and my office and the area corrections department decided to jump in and launch this program specifically for juveniles. I tried to begin the program in the local county jail as well, but that did not get a lot of positive energy. The program had a cognitive skills format and/or diversion style in its output. The program took place in the local juvenile detention center and also had sessions or skills classes with juvenile clients within the criminal justice system but not incarcerated.

When the program was launched, my first two juveniles were females who were not incarcerated. At first, this threw me off because of my assumption that I would get males in mass numbers given obvious statistics of black young males in the criminal justice system, more broadly males being overall more in jails and prisons. That was not my initial lot. But this proved to be very enlightening and productive because it helped me study and look at the cultural identity crisis from the standpoint of young African American females. The program in the juvenile detention center was mostly boys in those sessions.

Within my curriculum and the youth handbook, I had various program exercises, scenarios, and props to talk about this cultural identity crisis and negative and proper identity and its implications in how it can lead to improper views and behaviors. One main prop of the program was called Group Think, and during this part of the program, the students would have two images of African Americans either doing something specifically that was interesting, or they were celebrities or prominent people, and we would use these images to think and discuss identity.

On one occasion in the juvenile detention sessions, time frame around 2012, we were at a Group Think that had a picture of Jada Pickett. If you don't know who she is, she is an accomplished actress of African American descent, very pretty and with a beautiful light-skinned African American tone to her skin. Perhaps the fact that she is married to former rapper Fresh Prince and actor Will Smith might assist with a visual of who she is. In the picture, she had on a dress and had pressed or weaved long elegant hair. Next to Ms. Pickett's picture was an equally beautiful African American model, but she was of deep dark chocolate and native African skin tone. Also, she had descriptive African features and had natural thick African hair, wearing a white blouse. Both pictures were elegant, respectful, and easily well represented these strong, attractive, beautiful African American women.

The goal of this exercise was to see which one of these ladies would the young men choose as their potential date if they had the chance. That day, I had about five young men attending the program, and as it was often, I had a mixed group of races both of African American and Euro-American descent. In this case, three of the young men were African American, and the other two being Euro-American. So in a fun but serious way, the question was asked, "Who would it be that they would date?" All of them chose Jada Pickett without hesitation. That fostered some energy from the group of young men, some happy to just be doing something engaging. I then probed why, and while some might conclude that they chose

Jada Pickett because she was seemingly more famous given her acting prowess, there was one response that climaxed this exercise for me or highlighted what this exercise was all about and where I was seeking to go about the notion of identity, and the bigger aspect of the idea of a cultural identity crisis. That response came out loudly from one of the African American youth (a client I worked with various times via the public defender office) when I asked why any of them wouldn't date the just as beautiful but much darker and more natural model. He exclaimed a phrase that made me feel old, not having heard it, but he exclaimed, "She's busted." I knew where he was going but asked him why he thought that. He went on to explain in his teenage and urban way how Jada had her easily beat.

As infamously said, "Beauty is in the eye of the beholder," but in this case, this young man and others were associating her dark skin and natural hair as something that wasn't attractive or as attractive. What was more interesting about this young man's conclusion was that he was as dark as the model that was displayed in the picture. Not only that, but he was also rocking his natural African American afro. Naturally, I used this to open discussions on proper identity and relationship to why some juveniles were in the juvenile detention center. The depth of why this is so important couldn't be contained merely in this book, and the following experts will serve as champions of the depth of what this means. But when you take that thought and correlate it to self-esteem and various images of what many at-risk African Americans have heaped upon themselves and/or allowed to be placed on them as to who they are, this cultural identity crisis takes on life.

Along with that Group Think, there were others that were used that displayed what many stereotypically associated with what is authentically African American, such as the obvious entertainers and athletes. Those individuals were compared to nurses, doctors, lawyers, teachers, and mostly very prosocial individuals who were out of what many would stereotypically associate as hallmarks of African American culture. Not to, in anyway, disrespect athletes and entertainers, it was again amazing how the stereotypes of these people ruled the day as the best of what it meant to be African American and the images of other famous professionals (people like Colin Powell, Maya Angelou, Thurgood Marshall, Fannie Lou Hamer and many others this book could not contain, not to mention various local leaders and ordinary Joes and Janes) were not as desirable, liked or better said, even known.

Taking this to another level, we went into criminal behavior and prosocial behavior and its associations with various infamous minority prominent people and leaders. Many of these juveniles were so comfortable with criminality and its normalization that they often chose more negative examples than positive examples.

This cultural identity crisis, among other dynamics I propose, is so entrenched it must be unpacked and dealt with at all therapeutic and corrective levels, or efforts at behavioral change will fail. I gave a basic framework of why I conclude this is a viable issue in my work. But to adequately understand what this is all about the following theories and sociological anchors from research should be understood.

The Soul Wound

The idea of "the soul wound" is a key concept that sheds light on this notion. Clinical psychologist Dr. Eduardo Duran is an authority who provides perspective on this dynamic. Dr. Duran has authored *Native American Postcolonial Psychology, Buddha in Redface,* and *Healing the Soul Wound: Counseling with American Indians and Other Native Peoples.* His explanation of "the soul wound" is described as follows:

> The "Soul Wound" is essentially physical, psychological and spiritual damage which is the direct and residual result of the mass genocide and colonization by Americans. The "Soul Wound" is the result of the shameful history of persecution of American Indians which continues to this day to be propagated by all of society. This essentially means that the trauma of over five hundred years of oppression has been instilled and passed from

> generation to generation. This is not to suggest that it is a genetic ailment only that it is passed from parents and other family and friends on to their offspring, through the demonstrated behaviors observed by the child. The fact that the Holocaust committed against American Indian people has yet to be acknowledged by most of the world and certainly not the United States remains a principle impediment to the healing process.[41]

Dr. Sousan Abadian is another authority on this subject. Her biography includes MPA in International Development from the John F. Kennedy School of Government, Massachusetts, in the anthropology of social change and development, and a PhD in political economy and government from Harvard University. Dr. Abadian is known for her research with the indigenous communities of Alkali Lake and in dozens of other indigenous communities in New Mexico, Arizona, Montana, Minnesota, Alberta, British Columbia, and Manitoba. Her synopsis of "the soul wound" is described as follows:

> [Soul] wounds are both deep and widely shared in a traumatized society…they are typically the fundamental reason why such cultures cannot develop economically, socially, or politically until they address collective trauma and begin to heal it. Defeating a people has as much to do with destroying their sense of purpose—their confidence in their worldview and meaning system—as it does with physical conquest… adding that traumatic stressors engender in the victim characteristic feelings of deep violation and hopeless impotence in the face of violation.[42]

Historical Trauma

Historical trauma is a newer concept comparatively on the practical social modality and methodology scene. But it has grown with a lot of traction and practicality in the last decade or more. In its basic form, it is when you can see a collective trauma over a group of people that has been adjacent through a chasm of historical events.

Public health expert Dr. Michelle Sotero describes it this way within a public health concept, "The premise of this theory is that populations historically subjected to long-term, mass trauma—colonialism, slavery, war, genocide—exhibit a higher prevalence of disease even several generations after the original trauma occurred. Understanding how historical trauma might influence the current health status of racial/ethnic populations in the US may provide new directions and insights for eliminating health disparities."[43] What is significant is how this is correlated to disease, noting in its origination three frameworks: social epidemiology, political/economic theory, and social/ecological system theory.

In its origination, this concept, like the concept of the soul wound, was found in the Native American world via the indigenous peoples of North America. In some of its earliest thoughts it has been described as a cultural post-traumatic stress syndrome (PTSD) standing upon two preexisting foundations: historical oppression and psychological trauma.[44] As previously noted, it was popular in the health sciences and now found much more root in the mental health world.

Cultural Trauma

Cultural trauma is synonymous with historical trauma but emphasizes the impact of trauma on a culture. As described, it is when a culture of people feels they have been subjected to horrendous events that have left indelible marks on group consciousness, and this dynamic forever impacts collective identity and fundamental practicality.[45]

Post-Traumatic Slave Syndrome

More specific to this focus is a contemporary and innovative concept that has received prominence. That is the notion of the post-traumatic slave syndrome championed by the dynamic Dr. Joy DeGruy. This idea pinpoints the specific historical or cultural impact that slavery has had on a group, African Americans.

For those within the mental health business, this is a fascinating look at what would seem to be very obvious for those who understand mental health. This alludes to a cultural PTSD. The best example of PTSD in our current society is via the military. It is widely known of PTSD that many soldiers deal with this residual trauma within the United States, and thankfully, our country is working on this issue to assist our brave men and women who have dealt with very extreme circumstances in the defense of the United States, and more importantly how that impacts their lives of service after the military. In that same thought, PTSD is much broader in its impact on all extreme dynamics that cause trauma, and of course, there are varying degrees of this issue.

Dr. DeGruy's theory seeks to unfold as a collective impact on a culture. In a very practical manner and well-researched, she has concluded on the obvious trauma of slavery and that it still impacts African Americans today. While noting the obvious, she speaks about adaptive survival behaviors that we still see in today's culture. Also, she coupled that with the unfortunate dynamic of a particular absence of the ability to heal.[46] This research and ideal is acutely telling as it relates to disparities in the criminal justice system.

In total, in its basic and rudimentary formation, and too much for this context to do these theories complete justice, the soul wound, history trauma or cultural trauma, and post-traumatic slave syndromes are collective pain or oppression over a long duration of time that impacts fundamental worldview and life practicality. In the sense of the focus of this book, bring that back with the cultural identity crisis concept, specifically bringing that back in within the criminal justice system's historical overreach into African American culture, among others. Further, rehash the recent race issues of our time, as you will see a different light on the problems America has been facing along these lines and more importantly within the framework of criminal justice reform.

Racial Identity Development

From a standpoint of moving forward and how to address the previous concepts mentioned (the soul wound, historical trauma, cultural trauma, and post-traumatic slave syndrome), the concept of *racial identity development* is an essential factor that validates the notion of a cultural identity crisis but more importantly provides a structure to assist with the "what next" or objectives to add into what personal, programmatic and policy-oriented change would look like. This theory provides a way to address this topic in a holistic manner and strength-based methodology.

Psychologist Dr. William Cross is the foundational authority on this subject. His work and research "The Stages of Black Identity Development: Nigrescence Models" and various other research, develops and expounds on the idea of racial identity development. Cross identifies the following five stages of identity development:

Preencounter

> The African American has absorbed many of the beliefs and values of the dominant White culture, including the notion that "White is right" and "Black is wrong." Though the internalization of negative Black Stereotypes may be outside of his or her conscious awareness, the individual seeks to assimilate and be accepted by Whites, and actively or passively distances him/herself from other Blacks.

Encounter

This phase is typically precipitated by an event or series of events that forces the individual to acknowledge the impact of racism in one's life. For example, instances of social rejection by White friends or colleagues (or reading new personally relevant information about racism) may lead the individual to the conclusion that many Whites will not view him or her as an equal. Faced with the reality that he or she cannot truly be White, the individual is forced to focus on his or her identity as a member of a group targeted by racism.

Immersion/Emersion

This stage is characterized by the simultaneous desire to surround oneself with visible symbols of one's racial identity and an active avoidance of symbols of Whiteness. As Thomas Parham describes, "At this stage, everything of value in life must be Black or relevant to Blackness. This stage is also characterized by a tendency to denigrate white people, simultaneously glorifying Black people..." As individuals enter the Immersion stage, they actively seek out opportunities to explore aspects of their own history and culture with the support of peers from their own racial background. Typically, White-focused anger dissipates during this phase because so much of the person's energy is directed toward his or her own group and self-exploration. The result of this exploration is an emerging security in a newly defined and affirmed sense of self.

> ## Internalization
>
> While still maintaining his or her connections with Black peers, the internalized individual is willing to establish meaningful relationships with Whites who acknowledge and are respectful of his or her self-definition. The individual is also ready to build coalitions with members of other oppressed groups.
>
> ## Internalization-Commitment
>
> Those at the fifth stage have found ways to translate their "personal sense of Blackness into a plan of action or a general sense of commitment" to the concerns of Blacks as a group, which is sustained over time. Whether at the fourth of fifth stage, the process of Internalization allows the individual, anchored in a positive sense of racial identity, both to perceive and transcend race proactively.[47]

Practically, Dr. Cross's work became more understandable to me when I had the pleasure of working on my graduate degree under the tutelage of Native American educator Dr. Tom Peacock. In my discussions with Dr. Peacock, he gave me a different edge on the same notions. In his book *To Be Free-Understanding and Eliminating Racism*, he unfolds this understanding of racial identity development in how it often emerges in youth:

> As we enter adolescence, the physical differences we notice in people become more important to our developing sense of racial identity. All teens begin asking the same question of themselves; Who am I? However, young people of color take this a step further and ask: What does

> it mean to be Ojibwa? Dakota? Hmong? Black? Korean? Who am I racially?
>
> Why do they ask this? Because this is how others see them. Often when white adults see a teen who happens to be black, they think "black teenager." Many times, a teacher, regardless of his or her own racial identity, sees a group of Native teens, they think, "Native kids."[48]

In my study of this topic, I found the work of former Spellman president and psychologist Dr. Beverly Tatum to be the best in explaining racial identity development and the contemporary ideas on how to work with this issue. In her book *Why Are All the Black Kids Sitting Together in the Cafeteria*, she displayed this concept in a very user-friendly way that unfolds in most high school lunchrooms. Her developments are a useful conceptual picture of what this means. The following are some important objectives form her work:

Identity Development in Adolescence

> As children enter adolescence, they begin to explore the question of identity, asking "Who am I?", "Who can I be?" in ways they have not done before. For Black youth, asking "Who am I?" includes thinking about "Who am I ethnically and/or racially? What does it mean to be black?"

Racial Grouping

> Racial grouping is a developmental process in response to an environmental stressor, racism. Joining with one's peers for support in the face of stress is a positive coping strategy. What is problematic is that the young people are operating with a very limited definition of what it means to be Black, based largely on cultural stereotypes.

Positive Self-Defined Identity

> Cultural identities are not solely determined in response to racial ideologies, but racism increases the need for a positive self-defined identity in order to survive psychologically. To find one's racial or ethnic identity, one must deal with the negative stereotypes, resist internalizing negative self-perceptions, and affirm the meaning of ethnicity for oneself.[49]

The previous hypotheses have been briefly addressed to highlight or give foundation to the idea of a cultural identity crisis and, more vividly, how massive the undergirding of why disparities exist in the criminal justice system. These shed a colossal light on disparities and why they exist from a different point of view. As mentioned earlier, these are not the main headliners when it comes to the discussion of criminal justice reform. In my professional opinion, this is the current unfortunate reality. Just this briefing on these topics should be a call to action to go deeper.

With these theories as a bedrock to my notion of a cultural identity crisis within most minority lives within the criminal justice system, it will help to briefly discuss a couple of other facets of minority identity issues to open a greater idea of why this is so important. Most of these aspects are well-known and seen in what the "normal" life of a minority individual would be; however, within the at-risk mindset and upon the foundation of the previous, they take on a whole new meaning within criminal justice work.

Ethnic Racial Identity (ERI)

The concept of ethic racial identity (ERI) is contemporarily more recent and focuses on identity development from a racialized standpoint. It is another aspect of this subject matter to consider within this context. Dr. Tiffany Yip of the Fordham University psychology department describes that ERI specifically finds its development from prejudice, oppression, and discrimination. She further notes in the article, "Ethnic/Racial Identity—A Double-Edged Sword? Associations With Discrimination and Psychological Outcomes," the following,

> ERI is considered to be a multifaceted constellation of one's feelings, thoughts, and attitudes related to membership in an ethnic/racial group. ERI includes both the overall importance of ethnicity/race to one's identity and feelings about one's ethnic/racial group membership. Researchers have ascribed a universal developmental process across diverse groups (e.g., African Americans, Asian Americans, Latinxs), focusing on the feelings, thoughts, and behaviors associated with exploring the meaning of ethnicity/race, as well as psychological feelings of connectedness and commitment to one's group. It is also understood that although family, peer, school, neighborhood, and societal contexts impact how ERI develops from adolescence to adulthood, ERI remains relatively stable from one situation and one day to the next. At the same time, the psychological salience or relevance of that ERI changes across situations and days depending on characteristics of the immediate context.[50]
>
> ERI is fully understood with the development of adolescent ethnic and racial identity.[51] ERI impacts belonging to a particular group or groups, identification with shared values, and it plays a larger role among minority youth because they experience the contrasting and dominant culture of the majority ethnic group.[52] This is very important for minority youth because it is a resource for psychological well-being.[53]

All Things Considering

The goal of this chapter was to provide underlining context to underscore the depth of what identity means and various aspects that impact minority identity, worldview, and behavior. The scholars mentioned and their various theories and concepts are but a scratch of the surface but give an understanding of the delicate nature of identity and then the powerful impact of identity when unfortunately linked with racism and its residuals. When speaking of the soul wound, historical trauma, cultural trauma, post-traumatic slave syndrome, racial identity development, and ethnic racial identity, these references are used to describe African Americans and can be referenced for Native Americans and cultures who were historically oppressed in America.

However, these concepts take on greater meaning when you consider the disparities of black and brown lives in the criminal justice system coupled with its own trauma and its historical impact. These ideas shed greater light and should bring about an understanding that this issue of the unfortunate and historic partnership of minority lives with the criminal justice system is far deeper than the current American criminal justice structure has a grasp of. These ideas are addressed with respect to those minorities that frequent jails, prisons, probation caseloads, and courts. Hence, the need to understand this notion of a cultural identity crisis in collection with all the frontend advocacy and policies to change the problems in criminal justice. Also, and further inside criminal justice, the need to direct all efforts at corrective action, behavioral modification, and treatment to take full account of a cultural identity crisis and the various theories I briefly covered. These many thoughts and ruminations must undergird modalities and policies focused on changing the plight of minorities in the criminal justice system and destroying the horrific tide of minorities being overrepresented. As we now go further, we will contemplate how that practically can play out.

CHAPTER 7

The Dissenting Opinion

Some of the most enjoyable and coolest work I've done in criminal justice has been the privilege of working with at-risk and high-risk youth as a youth counselor, juvenile residential supervisor, and juvenile program manager. I've had the pleasure of working as a substance abuse youth counselor, shelter, and group home counselor, as well as supervisor of a juvenile sex offender program, intensive juvenile behavioral program, and a juvenile shelter program. For those who have had this type of experience or as a mental health professional, case manager, or youth counselor, one of the main goals among the focuses of treatment plans, cognitive restructuring, behavior modification, therapy, family therapy, reentry/transition, and the best least-restrictive normalization (fun in other words) you can provide, is milieu management among the family of clients on that unit. As you do this, seeking to keep various aberrant lives focused on behavior change and growth, you are sensitive to the fact that truly one rotten egg can spoil the dozen.

One of the things that has amazed me about this work is that you can have the worst-looking client on paper or per their life dynamics and criminal record, but within the residential process, that juvenile can be the best person ever and, within the program, can see the most progress. Also, on the other hand, you can have the most docile kid, a well-presenting demeanor, with minimal issues and a criminal record, and you know the story: that kid can be the worst ever in terms of behaviors and problems in the treatment program.

Years ago, when running the juvenile shelter program, my program was on the verge of accepting "Jackson" (fictitious name) to the program. He was one of these latter-described kids that presented well. Jackson had the horrible criminal family dynamics that most kids had. Also, he had concerning crimes in his past but nothing to the level that would be perceived as difficult. During that time, I had a great unit of competent and fun staff and the juvenile milieu was outstanding. I can't say enough about that team of youth counselors I had then. It was truly a dream team. The group of juveniles we supervised and managed or taught in a treatment context was typically at-risk or high-risk, with significant and tough dynamics in their life and family that were typical motivators to criminality (such as what the ACE's study reveals), or they had criminal issues and/or criminal ties. Most times, it wasn't them who were the criminals as much as it was the disadvantages, environment, and family they grew up with and around. In this regard, we were on notice of what could happen, and as said with the "Dream Team," the unit ran well.

Jackson was accepted to the program, and initially, he did really well. However, the "honeymoon period", a term we often used for the first days of a referral to a program, couldn't have ended more sudden. It wasn't soon after he joined the program that we had kids fighting and inciting madness on the unit. It was a tough situation for the staff. The interesting issue was Jackson was never in the fights or unit foolishness. It was hilarious (now speaking from a distance). But he displayed this obstinate will, cold demeanor, lack of respect for authority, and lack of a conscience or personal amenability. My staff and I constantly sought to redirect him and tap into what made him tick and wanted him to be a positive influence, but he was not locking into positivity and his negativity controlled the program.

During his stay, the program stayed in constant chaos. For those who have been in this business, you know as a supervisor, you are always "on call" or typically on call, depending on the dynamics of your program and staffing structure. As said, I had a great set of staff, so I literally wasn't needed at work. They were that good. But for this period, when I left work, either I was often coming back or on alert. While conscious that Jackson was the problem, my youth advocate instincts were to see it through, and of course, I thought we could help the young man within our program. However, I soon learned this young man was bound and determined to be that "evil" person, if you will, and his goal was to stir up the unit and incite criminal behavior. While these things cannot be best determined in youth as a definite diagnosis, what described this young man was descriptive of an antisocial personality disorder and, certainly, the conduct disorder tag. If not him at that time, it seemed he had the roots of such descriptions. For the purposes of the unit I was running at the time, we had little time to give this young man the therapeutic help he needed, with a hopeful psychological evaluation, individual therapy, and perhaps psychiatric and medication to offset potential mental health challenges. To use Drake phraseology, our treatment unit went "zero to one hundred real quick…," and we had to react quickly given the type of clients we housed and managed. Frankly, in the context of this treatment program, it simply was not going to change and grow with Jackson there. Additionally, we had to admit we couldn't handle the best interests of Jackson's needs and future.

Soon, he incited a brawl and his posse of criminal disciples in unified opposition to authority on the unit to a place where we had little control. I probably need to add here that this was a treatment program and not a correctional program, so by design, we were not equipped, nor should have been, to handle this in a physically confrontational or retraining manner as a juvenile correctional facility. We had tools in our shed, if you will, such as what was famous at the time, the Mandt system of behavioral control. But our unit was skilled in verbal de-escalation and milieu management as a result of well-built relationships and treatment/therapy-oriented focuses, and physical redirection was a last resort. Well, indeed, we were flirting with the last resort, but as said, Jackson wasn't doing anything physically. He was the humble "puppet master." Again, looking back at this, it seems hilarious that this young criminalized mastermind, or "Dennis the Menace on steroids," was that powerful. On this day, we had to call law enforcement to have this juvenile removed. While in the program, this juvenile never threw a punch or did any overt things, such as damaging property or anything that caused major harm; however, his criminal streak was legendary in my history of work with juveniles, and his negative energy and his way of generating negativity and a lack of respect of authority crippled the treatment unit I was running. Nope, he classically "didn't do it," but his loyal band of followers…they would cause major harm.

Jackson, from my last review, was still in prison for crimes he committed well after his placement into this specific program. After working with him and discharging him from our program, there was no question in my mind professionally that he would have a life of crime and the consequent need of the criminal justice system to override and monitor his life.

Jails and prisons are built for a reason. Some would debate the contemporary version of such, especially the idea of privatized incarceration and the understandable cries for the abolition of prisons. Without question, I would be among them pushing against the idea of privatizing corrections and abolishing the prison movement. I would agree with abolishing them as they philosophically, practically and programmatically exist and revamping them to something new. But there is no doubt a need for jails and prisons under city, county, state, and federal control. There is no question America needs strong law enforcement, courts, judges, prosecuting attorneys, probation, parole officers, and various correctional officers and staff. Call it an "is what it is," a "necessary evil," or just a societal reality equation. Sadly, these systems are needed. The idea of criminal justice reform and change is amazingly needed, but any idea of dismantling the need for these worthy careers and their purposes or notions, like the idea that got press for a while after the historic murder of George Floyd, yes, that idea of "defunding the police," frankness, and "keeping it a hundred" requires me to suggest or scream, such ideas are straight asinine. Being a part of the public defender family, I can boldly attest that we do need punishment or corrective action and its place in deterring crime and keeping communities safe. While I would argue behaviors have roots, and if we can get at the roots, we can change the behavior, the truth is, in my opinion, an "evil streak," if you will, is in some individuals exists (certainly, more therapeutically and descriptively categorized), and incarceration is the only true deterrent that will nullify criminal behavior and support public safety for some individuals. This is not an anti-therapy, treatment, and mental health statement, nor is it a support for police violence, violent prisons, or to sanction the continued horrible and historic problems in criminal justice. It is to say that we need these systems. Yes, we need the criminal justice system, but the thought should be, and certainly post-Floyd 2020, let's get it right. These systems need to vastly improve, and cultural disparities are a historical, systematic, ugly, or morbid blemish on these systems that must change yesterday!

In this thought, it is good to fact-check some sort of my bold notions or we are in need of a reality check in regards to the book's premise. Why this sort of thought? Is it needed? Why now? If you do the crime, you should do the time, right? Jails and prisons keep our communities safe, and those who are in there deserve to be, right? In deference to "keeping it real" or "keeping it a hundred," let's go there on various levels on this whole idea of looking deeper at this so-called cultural identity crisis.

Crime and Punishment Works…Right?

As I mentioned earlier, jails, prisons, punishment, or punitive measures are a "necessary evil," or admittedly, it's a necessary foundation for any reputable and successful city, state, and country. As much as many harp on the criminal justice system (including myself), many would attest that the criminal justice system is what woke them up personally and got them on a good track in life. It's a place where someone finds sobriety, consistency, order, tools, and even education to better their lives. Of course, I'd be wrong to say that the justice systems of our country don't keep our streets safe and provide for a necessary order for a functional society. Some would suggest, at its worst, it is an imperative deterrent to the misdirected and often evil tendencies of humankind. Therefore, the criminal justice system is a necessity. And I, for one, applaud many who lead, direct, and are on the frontlines of the criminal justice system daily to keep communities safe and provide law and order that is foundational to "the pursuit of happiness" and "we the people."

However, this is a huge "however," does the system work correctly? Has it been achieving its goals? I would assume many would say, "If the jails and prisons are full, at least these people aren't in the streets. And as crimes arise, so be it. Tough on crime always sells." As said, the criminal justice system is necessary, but its goals of "public safety," "corrections," and "rehabilitation" might be more akin to creating a "revolving door," its own club, and certainly subcultures in America. Toward the meaning of this book, prison's impact is so powerful when individuals are free of its grasp, they often want and feel more comfortable with prison life than what many might agree is normal life outside of being "behind bars,"; referring to the term mentioned earlier, "institutionalization."

In speaking about prisons alone, the criminal justice system's ultimate reality, is it effective? It is known while prison provides a place to ensure public safety while a detainee is held in prison, its overall impact in minimizing aberrant behaviors once someone is released from prison lacks positive outcomes. Recidivism is high among those who leave prison. Much of that is attributed to prison not having adequate programming or the ability to assist inmates in changing behaviors and while building a holistic skillset to acclimate to life after prison.

A report by the Brennan Center for Justice at NYU School of Law developed contemporary empirical evidence for incarceration's ineffectiveness tied to the reduction of crime. At that time, which was not too long ago, the United States was boasting about a researched reduction in crime as crime had steadily declined over the last two decades. Upon the foundation that the crime rate is half of what it was at its height in 1991 and violent crime fell by 51 percent and property crime by 43 percent since 1991, the Brennan Center for Justice notes their study about crime reduction:

> Using an economic model that accounts for the diminishing returns of extremely high levels of incarceration and includes the latest 13 years of data, the report bolsters past research suggesting increased incarceration had little impact on crime

> rates. Increased incarceration's effect was smaller than many previously thought. The report found that in the 1990s, it may have accounted for about 5 percent of the crime decline. Since 2000, the effect of increasing incarceration on the crime rate has been effectively zero.[54]

This 2015 referencing was a norm that does not take into account the up and down crime statistics after the pandemic of 2020, but it brings up the commonly used word in criminal justice, "recidivism." Not to insult the reader, but recidivism is when a felon comes back into the criminal justice system for more offenses after completing his/her said punitive sentence for previous offenses. The National Institute of Justice has a commendable definition of recidivism, saying, "It refers to a person's relapse into criminal behavior, often after the person receives sanctions or undergoes intervention for a previous crime."[55] "The quick and the dirty" on US recidivism is said well by Harvard Political Review's Liz Benecchi, as she notes a comparison that gives perspective, "Norway has one of the lowest recidivism rates in the world at 20%. The US has one of the highest: 76.6% of prisoners are rearrested within five years."[56] For those working in the criminal justice system, we know this isn't news. It's a consistent reality backed by research after research, and as we see, it's a said practical reality of America we work with daily.

One might ask, "If as you say, the criminal justice system is a necessary evil or needed for a civilized society, perhaps then the good outweighs the bad, or it is what it is?" I would suggest a big "no" to this kind of thought. These justice systems aren't highly effective and assure that there will be a subculture and assure that public safety isn't truly safe. The answer to this issue, in my opinion, isn't the absence of a criminal justice system but mandating an effective and culturally competent criminal justice system and making sure all efforts tend toward this powerful need.

Communities aren't safe if prisoners come out of prison doing the same things that got them there…at best and, according to the current criminal justice system, communities are safe only as long as many prisoners stay in prison. The issue then is, as said earlier, prisons are ineffective (not all but a majority) because they don't have competent and culturally competent programming, treatment, rehabilitative, correctional, and reentry efforts that truly lend to true behavioral change, not to mention being a force against the direct and indirect societal collateral consequences of having a criminal record. Benecchi, again, notes well of this issue through the eyes of a key issue in criminal justice, mental health,

> To put it plainly, unhealthy minds can't make healthy choices. The reality is 37% of incarcerated individuals and 44% of those in jail have been diagnosed with a mental health illness. Yet, 66% of prisoners reported not receiving any form of mental health care during the full length of their incarceration. With more accessible mental health care and substance abuse recovery for prisoners, they can be properly diagnosed and receive comprehensive treatment. With these revamped forms of relief and stabilization, the probability that those with mental illness relapse into destructive habits is far more unlikely than if they receive no treatment at all. Our justice system has an obligation to prepare prisoners for a safe and successful reintegration, a process which starts with a healthy mind.[57]

Crime and punishment, "tough on crime" efforts...does it really work? Well, somewhat...but in regard to the substantive and real issues, it is failing and must change course. When the cries for "defund the police" erected in 2020 while not plausible and an impediment to the idea of what it wanted, if you truly look at the failures of the criminal justice system, you can understand why such a phrase found root, not only because of bad policing but also because a criminal justice system that is a complete revolving door. The system doesn't need to be abolished as these cries for policing were pushing. It needs to change and be redirected. Part of that is understanding its long-standing problem with incarcerating black and brown lives and then a horrible inability to keep historic cultural "recidivism" and "institutionalization" from occurring.

The Yin and Yang of Research and Statistics

"Stats, who cares about stats. You can change them however you want to prove your point." In many cases, that is spot-on. While there is various supportive documentation to support the idea of a cultural identity crisis and its impact on criminal justice, there are areas of research that do not support it as a worthy notion for assistance in the correctional system. This theory is not supported by some well-competent and impactful authorities. The most notable part of my research at this point is that of criminologist, Dr. Ed Latessa. Dr. Latessa is a well-known figure on the topic of criminology. Currently, he is a professor and director of the School of Criminal Justice at the University of Cincinnati. Dr. Latessa has published many works in the area of criminal justice, corrections, and juvenile justice. With that said, I need to note that I'm not a criminologist nor have the clout of this distinguished scholar.

Within his seminal research, he has concluded that

- criminoginically racial issues do not matter;
- racial issues are not risk factors to assess change and effect change.

His findings were supported by his 1991 project, Community Corrections Partnership (CCP), 1991.[58] The era of his research was a key policy-oriented time for the evolution of mass incarceration. This was a multicultural day treatment project for primarily African American youth. Latessa concluded that culturally specific focused treatment has no greater effect than the normalized methods of treatment for all youth offenders. This was further supported in his 1994 report "Effectiveness of Culturally Specific Community Treatment for African American Juvenile Felons." In this report, he concludes that this particular culturally specific program was not better than the regular programming that any juvenile felon would get.[59] Alluding that cultural competency within corrections isn't a necessity.

From my study of this issue, the truth is we haven't had a substantial attempt across this nation to research and examine culturally responsive programs to thoroughly ascertain whether cultural competence in what I'm suggesting would truly work. Indeed, Dr. Latessa's work concludes it doesn't work, and respectful of his work and scholarly prowess, that is only one study of very few that have tackled the issue. Perhaps it's better said that such focuses haven't been a priority amid the issue of historic disproportionality within the criminal justice system. The criminal justice system all across America does not have in-depth, culturally specific programming. As Dr. Latessa's foundation work concludes, there might be reasonings as to why from a researched-based standpoint.

Post the George Floyd murder and movement, there has been a greater energy for this, and in various ways, it's being initially addressed on some fronts. Sure, it's now very popular to have culturally responsive mission and vision statements or even commendable objectives in an agency's organization plan. These are now like the latest clothing fad after the change movement of 2020 or an attempt to show "woke" ness or fear of public or legal reprimand if there isn't an organizational language, committees, trainings, policies, and focus groups on these topics. However, this is a call to go beyond making sure an organization uses cutting-edge terminology, department slogans, or hiring one staff to represent or pacify all the issues at hand. Naturally, I'm ascertaining that this can work and we will note anchors later on how this can be effective in having such emphasis in courts, jails, prisons, treatment programs, and probation efforts. At the very least, there need to be more studies that work on this issue to see if a culturally competent criminal justice system can break the strain of historic disparities.

The Folly of Mental Health Overreach

As a social worker in public defender work, I often work with those with mental health challenges or around the concepts and need for mental health intervention every day at work. It is essential in this work to adequately determine the foundation of behaviors to appropriately get at the roots of behavioral change. More importantly, if public safety is to be attained and maintained, proper mental health assessment and therapeutic intervention are a necessity. Otherwise, prisons would have to become places of permanent housing (some would say they already are). The growth of mental health has been a great avenue of discovery and growth within our world, and its continued expansion is desperately needed and required for any business, nonprofit, church, or correctional establishment committed to behavioral change.

However, on my own merit, I will emphatically say that it, like anything, can go way too far. What comes into thought is my previous question, "What do you do about behavior?" Having been a police officer as well, mental health means little when a threat to life (the person with mental health or potential victims) is on the line. At that point, mental health is secondary to the preservation of life first. This is a cold reality, but to some degree, there is no current answer to some of the vast mental health issues we see in criminals or criminal activity, and sadly, for many of those individuals in prison, the only way of keeping both the community and that person suffering from mental health safe is for them to be monitored securely. I'm not suggesting prison has to be that entity entirely. However, prisons and jails, as I have experienced them, need to adopt a different mentality about mental health while being the main agent of securing safety (a book on its own). Let the debates rage about this.

As a former professional in residential treatment, where mental health was very important to process and have successful outcomes, if the client's parents or the client themselves did not keep up with the medication regimen and therapy for diagnosed mental health challenges, it was a nightmare keeping the client out of the criminal justice process because they didn't or couldn't keep up with their mental health management. This is a challenge when correlating the need for mental health intervention when behavior gets in the way of keeping it as a central focus.

As we have delved into the idea of a cultural identity crisis and its implications for a disparity-riddled criminal justice system, there is no question it is being unearthed upon a psychosocial approach or psychoanalytic theorized approach. This is coupled with the anchors of sociology and psychology as well, bringing in the historical and cultural perspectives. But as its being theorized, it must be said, at least from this professional's standpoint, that this is not an excuse for behavior but an attempt to understand behavior and mostly then to evolve true solutions to aberrant behavior and behavioral patterns. In fact, from my vantage point, that is the totality of what mental health means: getting to the root of why certain behavior occurs and finding solutions, whether that means medical intervention, medication management, or a more holistic end to addressing a mental health complication. I would attest that a holistic or natural remedy to a mental health problem is much more desirable than not being dependent on medications or intense therapy. But as we know, many individuals struggle with various disorders and thus require pharmaceutical support and therapeutic support to assist with mental health management.

To stop short on mental health alone or the idea of a cultural identity crisis would be completely negligent and futile. Dr. DeGruy's post-traumatic slave syndrome, for instance, again leans on this idea of collective PTSD within a culture. However, if implemented as an assistant to behavioral modification in modalities, policies of law enforcement, courts, correctional structures, therapeutic entities, and day-to-day attempts to modify and change behaviors, it helps explain behavior and change behavior as an addition to other necessary efforts. It is not to explain away behavior or even to add to the continued lexicons of disparities. A mental health diagnosis, coupled with it the idea of a cultural identity crisis is much like a map to assist with behavioral change. If behavioral change is to occur and, in this case, disparities are to be lowered, the route to success must go through the path of understanding issues like mental health and this cultural identity crisis.

Full Circle on the Issue of Disparities

With all the various research out there and efforts toward building cultural competency, there are not many, or some might say any, entities that demand this type of cultural focus in the criminal justice system. *The Sentencing Project* mentioned earlier is a robust organization promoting reforms in sentencing policy, addressing unjust racial disparities and practices, and advocating for alternatives to incarceration. This competent organization is often referenced in my work field. It concluded that there are three recurrent explanations for racial disparities:

1. policies and practices that drive disparity,
2. the role of implicit bias and stereotypes in decision-making,
3. structural disadvantages in communities of color, which are associated with high rates of offending and arrest.[60]

This organization suggests the following ideas for racial disparity reform, drug law reform, mandatory minimum sentence reform, scaling back punishments on serious crimes, and adequate and regular trainings on implicit bias for those within the criminal justice business. These notions correlate well with the criminal justice reform goals previously mentioned and highlighted via the presidential administrations, starting with POTUS Barack Obama and beyond. These dynamics are somewhat consistent within the realm of other disciplines focused on disparities as well. I would courageously agree that these aspects are key to the journey as well. But of truth, these various dynamics do not speak to the cultural competency being espoused in this thought as a main framework from which to dispel disparities.

The Uphill Battle

In my field of work, it goes without saying that one of the most problematic issues, in my opinion, is the issue of disparities in the criminal justice system, the historic intentionality of such, and the horrible collateral consequence that has been heaped on various cultures for decades and centuries. As mentioned earlier, I professionally have grappled with this issue, and what continues to be revealed is the journey or quest to change disparities is woefully incomplete. This is said despite the many competent professionals and research tanks in the United States doing this work every day. This is now said, even after the momentum of 2020's George Floyd era seems to be dissipating although it was a pivotal moment to see vast changes in criminal justice.

As mentioned earlier, punishment or punitive measures for crime are a "necessary evil," if you will. When a police officer is looking down the barrel of an assailant's loaded gun, pointed at him or the public, historical trauma is not the first thing on a police officer's mind, nor should it be; swift action is needed. When a judge is faced with sentencing to prison for a seriously violent offense that has robbed a community, a family of a loved member, and a sense of safety within the community, the defendant's long-standing issues with mental health coupled with post-traumatic slave syndrome should not in most circumstances result in a probationary sentence that results in no prison, with outpatient treatment therapy and an ankle monitor. Further, while statistics prove that there are disparities within jails and prisons that doesn't mean that changing behavior isn't a significant public safety issue.

But even still, even against those thoughts that would conclude that race or the residuals of race are not a criminogenic factor or factors to consider within courts, jails, prisons, and probation caseloads, to address true change, there must be a cultural component that digs into deeper elements of behavior. The disparity issues are the proverbial "elephant in the room" of the criminal justice system, and as long as it is ignored, swept under the rug, or sophistically morphed into the newest research or phraseology or, even worse, championed by the liberal choirs for change substituting the singing for substantive change, disparities will continue to inundate black and brown lives. Cultural disparities have lit a continual and historic fuse of collateral consequences that are bubbling over time and crippling cultures. Despite many attempts to frame the "why" and advocate for legitimate dynamics, these have been incomplete in the full conglomerate of the disparity puzzle. Until disparities are significantly lowered in jails and prisons, America must commit itself to every avenue to change this un-American problem. Further, as mentioned time and time again, until the American criminal justice system recognizes its issue with race residuals and its implication and impact on the cultural psyche of minority offenders, this espoused cultural identity crisis and disproportionality will continue in America. Given the advancement in various methodologies, some methodologies that have been in position for decades within the think tanks and foundations of programming, the opportunities are available to ignite a more evolved attempt at changing this last leg of historic and expansive racism.

PART 2

Practical Implications
How Reform Can Evolve

CHAPTER 8

Methodologies Focused on Identity and Its Implications in Instruction, Treatment, and Corrections

As mentioned earlier, I was professionally impacted by this cultural aspect of my work, coupled with the historical disparities, so I decided to create a juvenile diversionary program focused on this cultural identity crisis. My goal was primarily to see if having a program bathed in cultural competence and positive identity development would work and, of course, with the addition of impacting lives within the criminal justice system. As I spoke, the program started out well. But I would be remiss if I didn't say while the beginning of the program went well, it wasn't soon after it's great beginning the local county's allegiance to the program ended, and they stopped sending their kids to the program, and further, I was not to continue the program at the local juvenile detention center.

This program was started in a prominent area of Minnesota. It began about eight years before the George Floyd murder and the consequent rise of an awakened civil rights movement of modern times, the call for change. I mentioned this because of the growth in energy for cultural responsiveness after that incident, and the movement might have embraced this program differently, probably still not enthusiastically, but with a different "energy." But before that, even amid horrible, recorded disparities for Minnesota and the obvious residual issues, not to mention this county and corrections program that boasted in their evidence-based practices and openness to cultural responsiveness, they would have none of this "critical race theory for criminal justice." While my program wasn't shy about connecting the dots as to how the criminal justice system has impacted black life and black identity via historical racism and its impacts, it wasn't critical race theory supported, and I give that in context to the fallout of this theory in public school systems of the 2020s; the fallout or backlash to CRT being taught in schools is similar to the reactions of that theory in public schools systems, but my situation was on a smaller and more administrative scale. Additionally, my program was cognitive skills related and was built to assist with behavioral change and to support positive foundations for prosocial behaviors after being involved in the criminal justice system.

Now before we get ahead of ourselves, there was no major scandal, no problems with kids attending, and no financial upheaval. To the latter point, I neither asked for nor received compensation for this program; it was a labor of love, research, and an attempt to build hopeful future alternatives for criminal courts to consider. It had nothing to do with competence and program materials or with its primary instructors, myself, and others that I brought in to assist with the program. Not to tout my own prowess, but having managed juvenile residential programs, I personally could run a diversionary and cognitive skill program with my eyes closed just based on my experience and training in that work. Thus, for me, it wasn't difficult to build the foundation of the program on decent cognitive restructuring frameworks. The cultural content was probably the most challenging piece as it was a new launch, with no criminal justice programs available to use or find wisdom from. It was a solid, culturally competent program built to assess and evolve around this notion of a cultural identity crisis while assisting juvenile clients in the criminal justice system. However, as said, love was quickly lost for my program, and I received the following "breakup" letter from the administration or "the powers that be":

> Dear Mr. Bailey:
>
> The purpose of this letter is to inform you that ——— Community Corrections will not

> support the presentation of the———[program] at the ——— Juvenile Detention Center. Additionally, we will not refer probation clients to the———[program].
>
> As we have discussed with you in the past, we are concerned with the message of the ——— [program] being less than positive in its approach and its reliance on promoting a view of offenders as being victimized by the system. We believe a more positive, forward-looking approach similar to that of the ——— [program] best compliments our agency's philosophy and is consistent with our purpose of creating positive change in our clients.
>
> We look forward to continuing to work with you in your role——with the Public Defender's Office.

This is quite the breakup letter, right? The love was gone! And this letter tries to allude to previous conversations about my program. There was nothing of the sort. It was just this breakup by text—no, it was a letter but felt like a text as no one in the administration ever talked to me face-to-face nor came to observe my program. This was all I received. Said in humor as I can look back at this. From what I was told by a friend who worked as a social worker in the county that hosted the program, this love letter went out to all the social workers and probation officers in the county. For sure, "I was on blast," and everyone knew I got "kicked to the curb." Again, so hilarious, now years past. But you must know the seriousness of this moment has not been passed on me.

For those who have been in this work and have worked along with these similar constructs and purposes, I'm sure you are reading many things into the reasoning for their refusal of my program. Your experience allows you to read between the lines and the confidential information I chose not to include. To be fair, I must lean on the hilarious idiom that I heard after I got divorced and in reference to the constant ways both spouse and others try to frame the causality of the divorce, that wonderful phrase is, "Well, there is her side of the story, there's your side of the story, and the truth is in the middle." While I'm sure this entity had its reasons, the key is what this agency noted about my program, "being less than positive in its approach and its reliance on promoting a view of offenders as being victimized by the system. We believe a more positive, forward-looking approach..." This was all due to the fact that we, as a program, we "went there" as a piece of the program to unpack racism and slavery's history and its contemporary impact on how African Americans live and think tied to the criminal justice system. We "went there" on this idea of a cultural identity crisis. It was built on the very notions already presented, my notion of a cultural identity crisis, and then the various other foundational and researched theories such as the soul wound, cultural trauma, historical trauma, post-traumatic slave syndrome, positive identity development, and ethnic-racial identity development. Of course, the purpose of our program was couched in a juvenile-friendly way, and it was buffeted by a therapeutic and treatment-oriented end that supported prosocial and positive behavioral change. There was no radical "Black Power" edge or any anti-American sentiment. In fact, one of the anchors spoke about building a sense of American pride amid all our challenges as a country.

That said, I must invoke my mother, grandmother, uncles, elders, and perhaps ancestors here because I think they'd give me some "keep it real" on this that would indirectly absolve the county from stopping my program. I'm sure if I said the same to them, they would say something like, "Boy, you a foow [fool] thinking them folks would support a program like that, you straight crazy..." To that constant voice in the back of my head, I say a hearty "Touché" to...it is what it is. However, my optimism and passion for change, well...I wrote this book, right?

As I mentioned, the program outside of the juvenile detention center had two girls to first come into the program. For this, we chose to speak about the challenges of African American women and the many aspects of life that remain a struggle for many women of color. The work is vast in this regard in relation to historical trauma and post-traumatic slave syndrome and too lengthy for this discussion, but the impact is massive. To support what we were doing, we brought in two former African American police female officers to speak from their experiences professionally and personally. What a wealth of experience, impact, and pouring of identity into these young ladies in the program.

My goal here in mentioning this episode of my professional journey as an African American man is not to show how good my program was or to vindicate my program or how horrible the system was in shutting my program down. I fully admit the difference in thought on said issues and the fact there is scholarly research that says approaching criminal justice in a culturally competent way, especially corrections, doesn't yield impressive results (the Dr. Latessa's of the world). But I would like to highlight the reasoning they gave "forward-looking and positive." Basically, to refer back to critical race theory (CRT) being a lightning rod in 2020, America's public schools, at the time, actually not too long ago, but just before the CRT controversy went crazy, this again felt like it was a CRT mission, if you will, and those in the administration did not see it as positive. As they explained, it wasn't positive or coming from a "strength-based approach." I don't want to fully speak for this department's reasoning for rejection (yes, I'm being nice), but "forward-looking and positive" is another way of saying we live in a "color-blind" society or saying that the past has no impact on the future.

Or it brings about a pang of organizational guilt and perhaps personal guilt. Yes, I said it, that the systems that are built to provide "corrections" and "rehabilitation" are falling short and still mimic or operate with the power and truthful assertions of Dr. Alexander's *The New Jim Crow*. While I understand that such a thing might invoke a measure of guilt to systems that are primarily led by Euro-American leaders, professionally, I would assume that anyone in criminal justice leadership would turn any notion of guilt into action to change the disparities issue. Moreover, if there is no movement for change and more horrifying if explained away in the guise of we want to be "forward-looking" or "strength-based," it's saying the fact that disparities exist is not a problem, it's normal for African American's to be in the highest percentage amounts in the criminal justice system. How scary… Dr. DeGruy in her work speaks of this well, in how it is far easier for the majority culture to erase the ugliness of the past and erase collective guilt toward a supported and, in my case, professionally disguised, explained, and celebrated historic cultural dissonance by the majority cultures.[61]

Could this be why disparities still exist in our current world in economics, health, education, and so on? How about why urban city unrest keeps going on year after year? Black Lives Matter? Why does vast diversity in jails and prison detainees continue to be an issue in a 2020-plus American criminal justice system? Could it be the guilt of the majority and the attempts to cover up historical reality by using professional "the past is the past," attempts to change the narrative with a positive spin, or their way of coloring it differently or less emphatically? Let the debates continue to rage but with some semblance of change in this very old story. I do want to continue to suggest we need to unpack the major cultural aspects of these issues, which I'm describing as a cultural identity crisis if criminal justice disparities are to discontinue and its many collateral consequences. Merely ignoring the past for the sake of "forward-looking and positive," when the criminal justice system has been a main, if not the main system to enact racism is a major mistake at the risk of continued disparities and an American culture of people being continually the fodder of its residual impacts.

I mention my journey in this area to underline what might be occurring nationally as it relates to having cultural competence in criminal justice system structures. Frankly, there are not many programs, treatment, or corrective in criminal justice structures across the United States that deal with culture as a main area of focus. It could be due to the research I've mentioned or this idea of needing "forward-looking and positive" programming. Some might refer to it as the need to have "strength-based" programming, and the idea of a defacto CRT isn't helpful in criminal justice work.

In my quest to understand the idea of a cultural identity crisis and its implications in the criminal justice system, I surveyed my current state and national landscape to see if any cultural competence was apparent in correctional and treatment modalities. My research also included contacting all state corrections departments of all fifty United States and getting information about what culturally specific programming they implement to battle the issue of disparities or to even address the concepts that are presented here. Simply said, there were only a few state correctional agencies that had culturally competent efforts toward disparities, and most were geared toward Native American groups. Few States had programming in the prison systems programming efforts. These answers were similar across the board, with nothing substantial within the criminal justice main frameworks: law enforcement, court systems, jails, prisons, juvenile treatment centers, and probation practices. This was not a shock, but I wanted to check on a surface level what is being done to go deeper with the issues of identity and concepts such as historical trauma and others.

Truthfully, just because there are not many programs in these main federal, state, county, and city frameworks does not mean there are no programs across the nation. In fact, my study to find federal and state programs could have missed programmatic efforts. Aside from that, there are various culturally competent programs in the nonprofit world and social service world that attempt to speak to these types of issues. However, what I want to highlight is that the criminal justice systems across America are not a place where culturally competent programs reside as a foundational imperative. This is a major problem if criminal justice is to be corrective and rehabilitative as much as it is punitive. This is a major problem if they house high disparities, such as 35 to 40 percent of the African American culture when it is only 13 percent of the United States population. This is a problem when there are other specialized efforts in criminal justice and corrections such as gender-specific programming, chemical dependency programming, mental health programming, programming set to the latest cutting-edge research, and on and on it goes, but again, nothing in mass speaking in policy and practice to for instance the cutting edge research of a post-traumatic slave syndrome via the work of Dr. DeGruy or the basics of racial identity development via Dr. Cross or Dr. Tatum.

As noted, the elements that are needed within the criminal justice field and in the discourse of this book are already set in much research and even within various fields today. I've also sought to note that a focus on the cultural identity crisis and its place in criminal justice disparities is needed within criminal justice reform efforts. With that in mind, I will seek to show a brief set of examples of what these foundations could exhibit within criminal justice policy and practice. This includes court systems, jails, prisons, law enforcement, corrective, diversionary, and treatment programming.

The foundation and professional prevalence of the DSM-5-TR is the gold standard in assessment and practice concerning mental health diagnosis. It is the world-renowned and respected concordance on mental health. It is used in various fields to explain and develop programming for those with mental health issues, including education, social services, medical fields, psychology, and even corrections when relating to mental health. It notes as a part of its foundations the need to address and understand cultural issues within the realm of mental health:

> Mental disorders are defined and recognized by clinicians and others in the context of local sociocultural and community norms and values. Cultural contexts shape the experience and expression of the symptoms, signs, behaviors, and thresholds of severity that constitute criteria for diagnosis. Sociocultural contexts also shape aspects of identity (such as ethnicity or race) that confer specific social positions and differentially expose individuals to social determinants of health, including mental health. These cultural elements are transmitted, revised and recreated within families, communities, and social systems and institutions and change over time. Diagnostic assessment should include how an individual's experiences, symptoms, and behaviors differ from relevancy sociocultural norms and lead to

> difficulties in adaptation in his or her current life context. Clinicians should also take into account how individuals' clinical presentations are influenced by their position within social structures and hierarchies that shape exposure to adversity and access to resources. Key aspects of sociocultural context relevant to diagnostic classification and assessment have been considered in the development of DSM-5-TR.[62]

This foundational statement of the gold standard of how America defines, understands, and categorizes mental health is a powerful example of what should color the criminal justice system A to Z from philosophy and practice in every courtroom, probation/parole department, law enforcement agency, jail, prison, public defender agency, treatment program, and reentry program. This is not only as it relates to mental health but also chemical health, court decisions, and all efforts at correction, behavioral modification, and reentry efforts. This could be rewritten in accord with this book's notion of a cultural identity crisis for every criminal justice agency, noting,

> As a criminal justice agency and court, we understand and adhere to the reality that sociocultural contexts shape aspects of identity and confer specific social positions and differentially expose individuals to social determinants that impact behavior. These cultural elements are transmitted, revised and recreated within families, communities, and social systems and institutions and change over time. Assessment, criminal justice and correctional programming and its desired outcomes should include how an individual's experiences, symptoms, and behaviors differ from relevancy sociocultural norms and lead to difficulties in adaptation in his or her current life context. Criminal justice practitioners

> should also consider how individuals' behaviors are influenced by their position within social structures and hierarchies that shape exposure to adversity and access to resources.

Of course, this is adopted from the previous DSM-5-TR reference, and thus, any credit would go to their amazing statement of conceptual framework, but such a statement was adopted and followed by mandate (very important as many agencies have vision/mission/purpose statements but not follow thorough) it would revolutionize the criminal justice system. In my professional opinion, it would lower the historic and continual cultural disparities in jails and prisons.

If this foundational lexicon in the DSM-5-TR sets culture as a major piece of mental health diagnosis and practice, how in the world, how in God's name… Frankly, could the criminal justice system not do the same in philosophy and practice or even be slow in the implementation of a similar focus throughout criminal justice? I admit this is an impassioned question from a professional frustration with the criminal justice system and its various leaders on every side. This is said even with those agencies and professionals that applaud and are "the choir" of such a foundation but fail to deliver on necessary change.

The Association of Multicultural Counseling and Development (American Counseling Association) is a holistic foundation for practical methodologies focused on identity and its implications in instruction, treatment, and corrections. This can be understood in a 1992 article where the Association of Multicultural Counseling and Development was grappling with culture and identity-based concepts as an organization. The article "Multicultural Counseling Competencies and Standards: a Call to the Profession" displays this progression of thought that the criminal justice structures of America should also grapple with and adopt. This is a document from 1992, in the thick of the war on drugs focus that grew prison populations and disparities. In the following segment is their rationale for the development of multicultural standards:

Another important factor that we need to recognize is that the profession of counseling, oftentimes, reflects the values of the larger society. References to counseling as "the handmaiden of the status quo" and "transmitters of society's values" indicate the potential sociopolitical nature of counseling. There are two political realities that counseling professionals must acknowledge and address.

First, the worldview of both the counselor and client is ultimately linked to the historical and current experiences of racism and oppression in the United States. For the minority client, he or she is likely to approach counseling with a great deal of healthy suspicion as to the counselor's conscious and unconscious motives in a cross-cultural context. For the White counselor or helping professional, he or she is likely to inherit the racial and cultural biases of his or her forebears. In all cases, the counselor, client, and counseling process are influenced by the state of race relations in the larger society. That the counselor is "supposed to help" or that counseling is "supposed to encompass" values and assumptions that reflect democratic ideals such as "equal access to opportunity," "liberty and justice for all," and "pursuit of happiness" may not be realistically reflected in the actual practice of counseling. Indeed, these lofty goals have often been translated into support for the status quo. When used to restrict rather than foster the well-being and development of individuals from ethnic and racial minority groups, it may entail overt and covert forms of prejudice and discrimination.

Second, counseling professionals need to recognize that counseling does not occur in iso-

> lation from larger events in our society. All of us have a responsibility in understanding the political forces and events that affect not only our personal but professional lives as well. For example, the changing demographics cited earlier are having a major impact upon our educational, economic, social, political, legal, and cultural system. With the increased visibility of racial and ethnic minorities in the United States, it seems that racial intolerance is on the rise. The increase in so-called "hate crimes" (murder, physical attacks, threats, racial epithets, destruction of property, and so forth) against minority groups is well documented. These reports are even more disturbing in light of the apparent erosion of the nation's civil rights law and President Bush's vetoing of the Civil Rights Act of 1990 and his opposition to the democratic version of the 1991 proposal. [63]

Within this segment, they cite things such as worldview, cultural tendencies, and oppression as issues relevant to the best methodologies in counseling for minorities. This brainstorming resulted in setting competencies and standards that stand firm today. The competencies and standards include the following objectives:

- Counselor Awareness of Own Cultural Values and Biases
- Counselor Awareness of Client's Worldview
- Culturally Appropriate Intervention Strategies[64]

As it relates to "rubber meets the road" practical aspects there can be many. The book *Crossing Cultures in Mental Health* notes various aspects in their synopsis of what this could look like in a criminal justice framework:

> In addition to such variables as perceptions, values, attitudes, and beliefs, culture is generally

manifested in a variety of rules and modes of conduct and thus impacts service practicalities. Failure to understand the cultural assumptions of a particular client may adversely affect therapist-client communications and overall service delivery. Areas of cultural diversity to which therapists should be sensitive include the following:

- Family Structure
- Important events in the life cycle
- Roles of individual members
- Rules of interpersonal interactions
- Communication and linguistics rules
- Rules of decorum and discipline
- Religious beliefs
- Standards for health and hygiene
- Food preferences
- Dress and personal appearance
- History and traditions
- Holidays and celebrations
- Education and teaching methods
- Perceptions of work and play
- Perceptions of time and space
- Explanations of natural phenomena
- Attitudes toward pets and animals
- Artistic and musical values and tastes
- Life expectations and aspirations[65] (Diane Koslow, 1989)

In addition to these aspects, other thoughts are listed in the book *Culturally Responsive Interventions: Innovative Approaches to Working with Diverse Populations*. Author Julie Ancis mentions five key practice components that affect treatment and advocacy: acculturation, violence and trauma, discriminatory practices, and culture-related stressors.[66] In total, these characteristics impact practical advocacy are vivid nationally and internationally and key in on the obvious need for growth in advocacy efforts for minorities and the aspects of historical trauma and racial oppression.

Despite previously mentioned findings of Dr. Ed Latessa, corrections and probation are beginning to debate and dialogue over issues of culture and identity within the corrections competencies. This is brought out in the article "Multicultural Competencies in Probation- Issues and Challenges":

> The first step in "cultural competence" is awareness of the predominant philosophical schemes of the other person's [client's] culture. These schemes include views of life and death, of conflict resolution, and of individual vs. family control. The second step is to maintain true respect for the other person's culture, accepting it as valid in its own right and equal in status to the customs of the dominant culture.
>
> The third step is to maintain an awareness of one's own limitations. Cultural competence means that the probation officer should be open to human differentness and enthusiastic about these differences.
>
> Fourth...cultural competence is client-centered learning, which means the officer admits what he or she does not know to the probationer. The officer should also request cultural information and seek out the probationer's view of the crime, probation process...[67]

The goal of this chapter was to display modalities among various that can be extrapolated in an attempt to evolve a philosophy foundation or the need for this foundation in criminal justice reform effort towards cultural competence or my espoused cultural identity crisis. I barely scratched the service as there are other examples of this idea. However, it was an attempt to show that there are maps already in place to implement quality movement in the criminal justice system toward going deeper with this disparities issue.

In summation, the information and research are conclusive about the cultural elements and their implications on minorities within structures focused on behavioral change. While there are varying thoughts and different conclusions, there is no dispute over the deep-rooted cultural aspects that affect mindset and behavior. It is very palpable because of a racialized America and its definite impact on many aspects, specifically for this discourse, how we act within that context, and how at-risk minorities are impacted by this process.

Further and accompanied by this idea of a cultural identity crisis, America has systems that have historically allowed racism to influence its practices, perhaps none more visible than the criminal justice system. As I displayed in my personal example, systems that explain away ways to address obvious disparities, their root in criminal justice, and the need to unpack said issues from a culturally responsive base. In total, this cultural piece is a major hurdle as it relates to changing behavior, treatment, and rehabilitation. This is a further obstacle as it relates to recidivism and working with at-risk minorities who seek to enter the workforce and get a quality education. This cultural identity crisis and its subsequent sway is far-stretching and will challenge the professionals and organizations focused on the criminal justice system. What is needed in future research and literature are more studies like Dr. Latessa's studies where implementation and results are taking place within cultural ideals in treatment and corrections. Practical enforcement of these ideals backed by assessment and qualified conclusions is necessary to conclusively build and evolve on the aspects of identity and how it can assist and better outcomes for at-risk minorities in the criminal justice system. Without question, the journey is noble and must be pondered and researched to help lower the plague of at-risk minorities in the criminal justice system and the crippling effects of its ramifications on culture and society.

CHAPTER 9

Practical Professional Outcomes

As previously mentioned professionally, I have wrestled with this idea of a cultural identity crisis through my work in various venues, particularly in public defender work. I see the evident labyrinth of identity issues that play into at-risk minority behavior, worldview, and even how they comprehend and work within criminal justice structures. What is unmistakably obvious in my occupation is that there continues to be a disproportionate number of minorities in the criminal justice system, and accordingly, this is a cancer to various cultures. It is further clear that while many aspects contribute to this cancer of a cultural identity crisis or its various other descriptive words, it is a vital contributor to disparities. Lastly and perhaps most importantly, it is clear that while there has been a growing understanding of the factor of culture and identity and its place in behavior, the criminal justice system has been slow to enact standards, competencies, and practical policies and programs to deal with this scary problem within a proportional majority of its clientele, African Americans, not to mention other minority cultures.

As this is somewhat of a young issue in the sense of its application, there needs to be further research and case studies on how to exactly deal with its varying obvious factors and undercurrents. Various professionals, from sociologists, psychologists, politicians, social service agents, nonprofit agencies, activists, advocates, and criminal justice practitioners, need to gather around this issue and with a passion for impact and change. With this in mind, there are contemporary models that exemplify what it means to tackle this issue of a cultural identity crisis with clientele in the criminal justice system, and these set an example of what can happen practically to assist with this issue and lowering the amounts of minorities in the criminal justice system. As I will expound, these very brief mentions of various practical realities are a set of examples that directly or indirectly impact this issue and, in my opinion, exhibit excellent prototypical disciplines of what should be occurring all across America.

I want to be careful to voice that there are many programs and professionals around the nation grappling with is issue and practically are on the frontlines doing this work. However, per my review and research, there are not many programs housed within the criminal justice system, specifically jails and prisons, focused on the idea of a cultural identity crisis or any culturally competent programming. Further, my conjecture is—and this will be my "if you hear nothing else, I've said, hear this" moment of this book—given the evident conundrum with disparities and its historical and cultural collateral consequences in the criminal justice system, standards, competencies, policies, and programs should be mandated to focus on this notion of a cultural identity crisis federally and within all state criminal justice systems. This is the "next step" to Alexander's *The New Jim Crow* and much other research, literal and visual/audio efforts to speak to the historical intentionality of incarcerating black and brown lives. Such action is a way to reverse the constant collateral consequences of the criminal justice on black and brown culture.

As I showed with the DSM-5-TR exemplary framework, all criminal justice structures should adopt a similar framework in philosophy, policy, and practice. Again, adopted from that framework, such programs should have a similar focus that reads,

> As a criminal justice agency and court, we understand and adhere to the reality that sociocultural contexts shape aspects of identity and confer specific social positions and differentially expose individuals to social determinants that impact behavior. These cultural elements are transmitted, revised and recreated within fami-

> lies, communities, and social systems and institutions and change over time. Assessment, criminal justice and correctional programming and its desired outcomes should include how an individual's experiences, symptoms, and behaviors differ from relevancy sociocultural norms and lead to difficulties in adaptation in his or her current life context. Criminal justice practitioners should also take into account how individuals' behaviors are influenced by their position within social structures and hierarchies that shape exposure to adversity and access to resources.

This concentration should not only be a vehicle of nonprofit organizations and social services efforts and scattered within the fight to end disparities among various professionals such as myself, but it should also be a requirement for all jails, prisons, courts, and probation/parole programming. Policymakers concerned about safe streets or public safety, behavioral modification, or corrective action, and the warriors for criminal justice reform should adhere to such foundations in their work and proposed laws.

This is the "call to action" on an evolved criminal justice reform and a stronger America that understands the crippling plight of a faulty criminal justice system and how it has amassed a major assault on cultures on cultures with long-lasting and generational collateral consequences. This is a call to true cultural competency within the criminal justice system. This call for action is not new, nor is this idea of a cultural identity crisis new. As said before, in research and practicality, my mere words to this are only a humble attempt at adding to the dialogue. The following are some real-world examples for all criminal justice and corrections departments.

The Association of Multicultural Counseling and Development

One example is the previously mentioned, the Association of Multicultural Counseling and Development (The American Counseling Association). This group has developed and demanded multicultural standards and competencies for their idea of a competent counselor and counseling agency. In viewing their competencies this agency focuses on the multicultural aspects of the client, making sure that in their ideal counselor practices, they take into account the totality of their client's cultural make-up. In this, they focus on words such as "culture," "worldview," "beliefs," and "attitudes" of the client. Within this same idea, they ask the practitioner, the counselor, to take into account their "culture," "worldview," "beliefs," and "attitudes" and how these aspects may impact their work. In total, the AMCD insists that counselors understand culture and adapt counseling practices because of culture.

This agency displays an example that there must be a proper policy foundation to deal with multicultural issues. I believe they also set a standard for any system that has frequent work with minorities. Principally, this should highlight the criminal justice system and its historic and glaring issues with minorities and disparity.

The Corrections Department Probation Officer Description

In researching various examples, another practical example of how this cultural identity issue is being addressed is through the development of employment positions that focus on it. An example of this is a simple job description once advertised by the Corrections Department of Niagara County, New York. This is an older position that can no longer be found as it is written here, but it still is emphasized in their probation department. It was a probation officer position entitled probation officer, minority group specialist. This position specifically focuses on the obvious issue of minorities in the criminal justice system and the need to be aware of meeting multicultural needs within the corrections process. The job description notes the following qualifications in the original posting of the position:

1. Completion of a major course of study in American Indian, Black, or Hispanic culture studies from a regionally accredited college or university, which must have included a minimum of twenty-four semester credit hours.
2. Two years of a close cultural association with American Indians, Black, or Hispanics, or a work association in a criminal justice setting that requires advocacy for or interaction with American Indians, Blacks, or Hispanics.

In recent view, it read as follows,

> A. Probation Officer (Minority Group Specialist) Under a special dispensation from the New York State Division of Human Rights, this title may be utilized in all municipal jurisdictions which have submitted to the Office of Probation and Correctional Alternatives justification that such position is needed to address the under representation of minorities in their respective local probation departments, and have received written approval from the Division for the establishment of such a position.
>
> 1. Distinguishing characteristics. Probation Officer (Minority Group Specialist) incumbents perform the same activities and tasks as performed by Probation Officers along with the additional responsibility of identifying and relating to the specific problems encountered by minority probationers and communities upon assignment. The caseloads for these positions may, to a significant extent, be comprised of individuals who need special attention due to the socio-cultural environments from which they come.

> Incumbents of these positions may provide insight which could enhance and increase county probation departments' special sensitivities, experiences and knowledge necessary to operate and to assist in the evaluation of local programs and service delivery to make them more responsive to the diverse and pluralistic populations which county probation departments serve.[68]

This agency's hiring practices highlight the fact that agencies need to hire competent minority staff or staff with a qualified specialization with cultures that are frequent in the criminal justice system. This is an exemplary model that is practical and aware of the fact that minorities overwhelm the criminal justice system and bring unique realities that must be considered in the treatment or corrections process. This is a model that is competent to understand and relate to the historical and contemporary racism adjacent to the criminal justice system. It is also excellent in realizing the identity factors that play into many at-risk minorities.

Social Service Programming

The Project Hope and Pace program of Olmsted County (Rochester, Minnesota) is another example of how multicultural policies or ethnocentric identity theory impact practices and policies. In my past work, I became familiar with the program and always remember it as a shining example on to address the issue highlighted in this book. This program embodies principles and programming that I contend the criminal justice structure needs to upgrade in its rehabilitative and treatment process. Former Olmsted County Social Work Supervisor, John Edmonds, was one of the original founders of this program, along with a staff of culturally specific case managers and social workers.

In an interview with Edmonds about his programs in 2012, when the ideas and brainstorming of the book began, he mentioned that the program is focused on African American families and youth and uses crucial methods or thoughts applicable to the notion of a cultural identity crisis. Edmonds did specifically mention the idea of a cultural identity crisis but spoke to the broader context of cultural competence and its need to be implemented in his system to combat disparities. These aspects highlighted other areas of positive support and the impact of the theory of a cultural identity crisis.

Edmonds identified the need for a foundational purpose similar to that of the AMCD's Multicultural Counseling Competencies. In this, he emphasized that his programs use procedures that are focused on African Americans and specifically issues of disparity in the basic social structures available.

Secondarily, Edmonds mentioned that his program has firm intentions to meet the needs of African Americans through competent personnel. This parallels the job description for the Niagara County Probation Officer Minority Group Specialist. Similar to this agency, this program intentionally seeks out and hires African American staff to assist with the purpose of his programs.

Lastly, Edmonds expressed the practicality of unwavering follow-through as it relates to African Americans in Olmsted County. He mentioned a common thought in his regional area that it's hard to find qualified African American staff. To this, Edmonds refuted that notion, pinpointing that it's about a commitment to follow-through with his purpose and going out of his way and making extra steps to find those African American staff that are available.

This program has evolved since 2012, but it still has a similar focus:

> PACE is a diversionary program for children of color between ages 5 and 12 reported to the child protection system for education-related issues. Deeper-end child protection services include foster care placement and court systems that often traumatize children and their families and put a significant financial strain on county systems. PACE diverts kids of color from the child protection system by offering front-end

> case management services that wrap around the needs of the family. Services include resources and referrals to meet the family's basic needs such as housing, medical, social, and emotional needs and those related to the child's educational well-being. Efforts are made to improve engagement between the child, their family and school. PACE offers both preventive and corrective case management services, not just for the child referred, but for all children in that family. Implemented with a budget of $174K to serve 31 children in 2010, the program has grown 300% in budget and has served 605 children along with their siblings and families between 2010 and 2019. PACE is managed by six full-time staff along with a program manager.[69]

This program is a social service program, and that isn't unfamiliar within social services and more broadly nonprofit programs nationally; however, there are few criminal justice and/or jail and prison programs that speak to this issue. The verbiage, research, and dialogue are there and has increased post-Floyd 2020, but the practical programming has not increased. There are simply few programs within criminal justice that mimic the idea and practical output of the Pace Program. As is shows with the program I created and was shut down, the criminal justice system is obstinate to having such a program, or it's just willing to allow the disparity issue to be a continual "elephant in the room" that isn't to be addressed. It stands as a glaring and exemplary example of what should be federally forced and mandated in state structures of the criminal justice system.

Specialty Courts

Specialty Courts or "problem-solving courts" have been a growing phenomenon in criminal justice since I've worked in the business. This would include specialty courts such as drug court, veterans court, and mental health court. Specialty courts differ from court to court with the premise of having a nontraditional court environment that speaks to changing the plight of continuous problematic issues. In this, the court works with individuals to see them through various challenges related to the title of the court. For instance, the state of Massachusetts has various special courts ranging from Adult Drug Court, Juvenile Court, Family Drug Court, Mental Health Court (also called Recovery with Justice), Veterans Treatment Court, and Homeless Court.[70] I previously worked in Arizona, a state the exemplified such courts. Pinal County, Arizona, provides a great definition of specialty courts:

> Specialized courts differ from traditional courts in that they focus on one type of offense or probationer. Specialty Courts are problem-solving court strategies designed to address the root causes of criminal activity by coordinating efforts of the judiciary, prosecution, defense bar, probation, law enforcement, treatment, mental health services, and social service agencies. Together, they maintain a critical balance of authority, supervision, support, and encouragement. Specialty Court programs are rigorous, requiring frequent drug testing and court appearances, along with tightly structured regimens of treatment and recovery services.[71]

The criminal justice system, in the case of specialty courts, recognized the need to focus on specific groups (mental health, veterans, the chemically addicted, the homeless) for better outcomes, better behavior, and better public safety, so much so the idea of specialization of courts was born. Admittedly, this idea is too radical to consider, let alone mention, but given the vast number of minorities that frequent and have frequented the criminal justice system since the birth of America, what about special courts that deal with culture, that deal with the specialty groups of culture that overload the system. The idea, for me, is even hard to imagine, but on the premise of specialty courts it does make some sense. Apparently, Australia has understood this. Note their description of their specialty courts,

> Specialty courts, designed to tackle specific problem behaviour and associated issues, have been adopted by policy-makers and criminal justice practitioners as a means of tackling crime related to drug dependency and mental health, reducing the over-representation of Indigenous offenders and reducing the incidence of domestic violence.[72]

In thought of the examples presented (not exhaustive by any means), a social service program, a policy-oriented organization, specialty courts, and a probation agency position dedicated to these issues…all having structures that can apply to focus on cultural competence, image again, the disparities issues within jails, prisons, courts, and probation caseloads. Image the issues that Alexander reveals in her aforementioned book, *The New Jim Crow*. Imagine all the energy and focus on criminal justice reform and the 2020 George Floyd movement for change. Then image programs like these examples are mandated and strategically spread through the criminal justice system and also adapted to the motif of courts, probation, parole, reentry, jail programs, prison programs, juvenile justice programs, staffing patterns, public defender systems, and various leadership hired to lead criminal justice entities. If mandated and implemented, this would be criminal justice reform at a whole new level, and I would dare say, be a truer version of reform and help drastically reduce the historic cultural disparities so powerfully entrenched and glued to the present-day criminal justice system.

My Professional Philosophy

As I will elaborate on later through my personal and professional life, I've established five anchors that should be a part of any jail, prison, corrections department, innovative court, and law enforcement agency that wants to really make a difference with disparities and address this notion of a cultural identity crisis. Those anchors are academics, belief systems, legacy, exposure, and opportunity. These anchors do not nullify the already safety and punitive restraints that exist throughout the criminal justice system. This isn't absent the idea of incarceration. It's an argumentation or evolution of how it works for pro-public safety outcomes and true behavioral change, not to mention the impetus of this discourse lowering cultural disparities in the criminal justice system. Moreover, if these foundations are at the root of every criminal justice attempt to change or correct behavior, I boldly attest there will be a lowering of historical disparities and a revolution to how the criminal justice system works.

Academics

As described by many current leaders, academics are a continual civil rights issue of our time. It is clear throughout the US that students of color are not getting a quality education while at the same time crowding the criminal justice system. This is portrayed in the achievement gap issue, which is a serious issue nationwide. The National Assessment of Educational Progress (NAEP) describes and defines the vital nature of this gap as follows, "Achievement gaps occur when one group of students outperforms another group and the difference in average scores for the two groups is statistically significant."[73] This is vital as African Americans and other minorities are achieving at lower rates than there Euro-American counterparts. Further, it is vital due to its correlation with minorities in the criminal justice system. Various reports and commentaries on the achievement gap, such as the NAEP, show while there has been progress with these issues, it still lingers at a domineering pace, in some areas of the United States not improving at all.[74]

Typically, clients with such educational issues are the clients who are thronging the criminal justice system. It is still a reality that 68 percent and above of those within American jails and prisons came in without a high school diploma[75]—some studies not 70 to 75 percent. It is clear that if youth do not receive a quality education, they are unequivocally behind in America and prone to crime. Youth within those critical identity years of sixteen to twenty-four who drop out of high school are 63 percent more likely to be incarcerated than those with four-year college degrees.[76] The correlation between a lack of education and incarceration is clear. Sadly, the correlation between the historical existence of minority cultures within criminal justice is clear, and a lack of education is a contributor.

Moreover, their identity and understanding of who they are is often skewed, limited, and counteractive to productive living. I don't want to suggest a total adherence to aberrant living, nor a nostalgia necessarily of crime being "cool," but indeed, there is often a holistic settling with the albatross of the criminal justice system and its ugly collateral consequences. At best, often, there is a depressive settling for how it can inundate a life and a culture.

To establish a proper identity in American culture, there must be an objective to help at-risk minorities reach their academic potential. At some point in American education, in the mix of racism and its perceived and real consequences, it strangely became not normal. This is in stark contrast to the fact that education was a vital foundation to African America life in times when slavery and overt racism existed at a high level. Education was so integral. As we know, it was outlawed by slaves for a period of time. Hence, enter again that long historical and racist arm of the criminal justice system and its collective collateral consequences. If at-risk youth add a stigma to being educated before the teacher even enters the classroom, there is a mammoth obstruction to teaching and educating at-risk minority students. The aforementioned book, *Multiplication Is for White People*, highlights this issue with minority identity with education.

Today, African Americans are more stereotypically known for sports prowess and entertainment acumen (of course, this is not true, but still, an overwhelming stereotype and spoken to later in this book) and then add in the consequent quest of young minority lives into these two arenas, the story must be told to at-risk and youth and young adults that their heritage is far beyond that. The 2016 award-winning movie *Hidden Figures* told of such a legacy of women and their educational expertise and impact in the world of America's historic battle to reach the moon in the 1960s. On a personal note, and I would venture to say many at-risk young people who grew up like me, we all didn't here of these types of stories in school. In my forties, I had to go to a movie theater to first hear about this. Mind you, it was a grand presentation, and my children no doubt were empowered by it. However, expand that thought to all the minority lives within the criminal justice system and then think of the identity they often brandish and are enchained by.

Time does not permit us to speak to the powerful impact of education, how it is a vital key to a successful life, and the fact those without it often never attain success. Statistics still bear out that minorities are less educated and do not value education as most of cultural peers. Likewise, as noted, minorities frequent the criminal justice system. These two aspects correlate in a diabolical fashion, and any system of change must understand this correlation and seek to address it. Education should be at the foundation of any criminal justice system venture. Within jails, prisons, and youth programs built to correct behavior, education should highlight all programming to the place where detainees leave jail and prison, as well as programming with knowledge and skills to get and maintain a career and prosocial lifestyle.

A radical thought: education, or specifically getting a diploma or qualified vocational skill/license, should be a prerequisite for any prolonged juvenile sentencing or sentencing for a young adult. This means that to complete a juvenile sentence for a major crime or when sentenced for a significant duration to be in programing or incarcerated, that youth must complete transferable education or vocational skill prior to completion of their "time served" or to complete treatment programming.

Or what about this thought? A landmark decision occurred in December 2020, and it was fully enacted in 2023, the full actualization of the Second Chance Pell Experiment Initiative. The United States Congress lifted the ban on Pell Grants for the incarcerated. This means any person in prison can seek a higher education degree in prison. While this is great news, this doesn't mean higher education in prison is balanced across America. Some states are strong with higher education models, and some aren't. How about a federal program and state programs that assure that any prisoner, upon meeting correctional requirements, is afforded the full opportunity to pursue vocational and higher education degrees that will be highly supportive once detainees leave prison?

All correctional programs should have this ability or the ability to link with an education institution to provide this dynamic. Radical indeed, but again, think of disparities, the deeper racial implications espoused in the book or otherwise, and all its historic collateral consequences.

Belief Systems

Belief systems are another imperative piece for at-risk minorities to develop a positive identity and, therefore, should be a foundation for standards, competencies, and practical policies and programs in criminal justice. By belief system, this means those beliefs that are anchors to behaviors. At-risk youth and adults, at their core, have this part of their lives usually shaken or shattered. At-risk minority youth deal with this further as an issue because of their racial identity development and the place it plays in their belief system.

In the process of growth beyond aberrant behavior, at-risk minorities need this anchor to support their growth. This could be their faith, their value system, their spirituality, or their worldview. Typically, this area can be avoided (more prominent in the juvenile arena) due to its potential to support religion and religion within the treatment and corrective context. This is clearly understood, given the separation of church and state and all the dynamics around this idea. But those in power or the majority race often have the real or perceived internal and external compass and worldview that is America.

The idea of this critical area is brought out in the qualitative study by Testoni et al., *The Value of Dignity in Prison: A Qualitative Study with Life Convicts*,

> According to Western culture, which is based on the value of dignity, prisons should

> provide concrete tools to prisoners in order to maintain their human identity and respect their personal values. Indeed, article 27 of the Italian Constitution asserts the absolute value of personal identity and dignity. As our study indicates, life imprisonment deprives prisoners of all these by destroying any dimension of existential values. All participants valorised the right to work, the right to health, the right to education and, above all, the right to love. Indeed, the penitentiary system should respect all these values, because doing so empowers prisoners to maintain family and emotional relationships as well as pursue education and the furtherance of job prospects and social reintegration, which are all values that lie at the heart of human dignity.[77]

Any contemporary view of American prisons and even the criminal justice system doesn't engender the value, worldview, or even the faith of human dignity and identity. The infamous trauma of the formerly incarcerated speaks of this. Moreover, the system is so set on punitive measures, retribution, and reckoning even in its wording and claiming of "corrections" and "rehabilitation," it fails, noting the trauma of its entities and recidivism of its outcomes. Despite that, the criminal justice system should be the ideal place where the penalized and incarcerated can reestablish positive and foundational worldviews, values systems, human dignity and identity, and even faith.

I don't want to assume the notion of "white privilege" in this context, but many worldviews and faiths are centered around the idea of the American dream and all it provides and has provided. This in itself can be a tremendous indirect motivator for prosocial and positive behaviors, indeed the idea of being successful. The minority at-risk identity and some would say minorities, in general, often don't have that association with America and all its residual benefits from house, home, family, education, and vacation, if you will. Racism and its impact have shattered that ideal, going back to the Kunta referencing. This is not to say it owns a dominant place and is an overreaching obstacle that a person can't overcome; that would be exceptionally false as both those within and without the minority cultures have overcome magnificent odds to be great successes. In a sense, it is the American story. However, the truth is that racism has put into the at-risk or minority psyche that this isn't a part of their foundation and worldview to succeed. This is massive and can be unpacked on various levels, but a healthy belief system as it was for African Americans during the time when blatantly African Americans were thought of as not a part of "We the People," it can take a person or a people to heights beyond current negative circumstances.

The criminal justice system needs to ascertain the fact that racism and further ramifications of at-risk life have ripped a sense of foundation for at-risk minorities. Many of these clients are born and nurtured without a compass to judge their lives and actions. A healthy belief system provides a structure for those embattled with criminality and its identity to change what has been normal and give meaning to prosocial living.

Further, a belief system gives at-risk minorities the ability to look beyond definite and certain negativity. There are many aspects that describe the negativity of minorities and at-risk minorities; these aspects are stressful on lives and cultures. For African Americans, black-on-black crime, lives defined by the criminal justice system, social and health disparities, obvious poverty, still existent overt racism, institutional racism, and above all those, in my opinion, the struggle for identity and a bolstered cultural and individual self-esteem amid these issues, provide a stressful and tense life. While there's been growth for African Americans, the resurgence of various levels of public racism post-Obama have been taxing on African Americans (and other minorities) mental and emotional health. Often, there is a common and collective depression and longing for individual or at least cultural value that speaks to our equating and valuable strength and contribution to America and the world. This is a daily tension for minority cultures; add this to the at-risk mindset, and you get an evolved depression, oppression, and reaction. A belief system in this context gives meaning where there is no meaning; it gives a ray of light where cynicism has declared there is no way out. It gives meaning to life beyond at-risk realties and provides the foundation for life and living successfully.

A strength of the African American culture has been the ability to thrive through these realities historically through the avenue of faith and an adopted worldview around suffering that includes laughter, art in all forms, innovation, and an indomitable will. This strong strength and worldview must be told in the criminal justice system as a historical element and further an agency of empowerment for young men and women to beat the odds.

I would be the first to say that the state getting involved in belief systems or spirituality is a sticky business, and it would be hard to develop properly. But at the very least, there needs to be a foundation for those empty of self to find what makes them look within and beyond themselves to carve out a prosocial identity with themselves, their culture, and their country to be productive. What avenue comes about, and to what faith or worldview would be an individual's place to adopt that? Regardless, there must be a fostering of that ability.

This is where belief systems are imperative. The amount of pressure that life can yield on a person, let alone racism and the ugly things it can do, must be predicated by a belief system that can explain, influence, and instruct proper behavior beyond it. Racism, in my opinion, is one of the ugliest sins or atrocities known to man. Indeed, its overt oppression of yesteryear and disguised authority contemporarily is hard-hitting on people of color. Far dangerous, in my estimation, is its destruction of minority identity and self-worth. There is a collective self-image issue among many American historically oppressed minority groups. This is a collective depression, I attest, because there is a loss of identity due to historical and contemporary racism.

Belief systems provide an anchor to escape this collective depression and self-image issue and further give wealth to self and culture that may not be commonly experienced. At-risk minority populations must build a belief system that reinforces there individual and cultural values. While difficult in the state-funded correctional and treatment process, corrective and treatment services must foster and allow the element belief systems to be cultivated and supported in the rehabilitative process.

A radical thought: As I've seen, most criminal justice entities are open to allowing their clients to seek out whatever prosocial faith or worldview they desire. While a touchy area, I believe it can be fostered more and as appropriate within the criminal justice system. Many programs promote cognitive skills to address criminogenic thinking, programs in my day such as *Thinking for Change* and *Truthought* (there are various other programs). While needed, what about fostering an identity and ethic that helps youth and adults in the criminal justice system to build a value system for those behaviors, a value system that, in the face of challenges and unfortunate obstacles to stay law-abiding, pushes them to identify with and choose positive pro-social behaviors that support to productive and crime-free lives.

Legacy

Legacy is another important piece in the journey toward building a healthy identity. To be able to properly deal with life beyond racism, the legacy of racism, real and perceived racism, must be expounded graphically and purposefully. Racism is real and has played a significant part in our society and criminal justice system. Criminal justice and treatment practitioners cannot ignore the fact that the criminal justice system has been one of the main historical structures used to enact racial policies or, better said, keep racial policies and practices in force. The criminal justice system must understand how this historic past is often a barrier in the correctional and treatment process.

Further, the system must understand the impact of racism on society and, frankly, most of their clientele. They must come to understand the impact of generations of cultural incarceration has impacted the identity of its at-risk clientele. To many or most, the criminal justice system and all its facilitators are synonymous with racism. Whether legitimate or not, a competent criminal justice professional understands this and has developed skill sets to deal with this reality.

As well, and perhaps more difficult, there is no denying the fact that racism is often used as a crutch with many at-risk clientele to the place where it affects correction, rehabilitation, and treatment. Quite simply, this must be hit head-on in the treatment process to expose it and encourage a posture to move beyond it.

Working with the criminal justice system, I am one of very few African American men and minority professionals in the criminal justice system comparatively. As I have this opportunity to work and train others within this business, I experience the plethora of actions and reactions of those ignorant of the racial implications of crime and justice; this would include those trained to work in these fields and the clientele themselves. Many situations come to mind, but none more vivid than an experience from a former colleague who was an assistant public defender and culturally a native of Western Africa. In one of his cases, while representing and African American client, he was verbally butchered as a "sellout" lawyer, basically called not authentically African American due to not getting the outcome that this client wanted nor advising them in a way in which they thought they should be advised. For most American minorities, this isn't a surprise; "sellout" is still a vivid dynamic in post-Obama America. However, it underscores the identity issue, its linkage to age-old racism, and the fact that professionals in this criminal justice of all cultures have to deal with this in order to be successful.

Another constant issue I face as one of the few who work with the prison population is that many times, my white colleagues have barriers working with clients all because of race. Within the public defender's office, I have worked and facilitated trainings. I have been privileged to work with some of the most competent, experienced, compassionate, understanding, non-racial Euro-American people I've ever worked with. These people have a collective heart for people like I've never seen. But, even still, race is a barrier for most of them when working with at-risk minorities. This doesn't mean they are not affective; it means they may have a larger hurdle to jump to represent our minority clientele. Yes, all because of race and its implications.

Without question, being an African American, having experienced the journey of our clientele in one way, shape, or form most, a majority of the time, I don't have the same hurdles to climb to work with our clientele, again just because of racial implications. This can prove to be positive or negative, but it's an unacceptable dynamic of working within the correctional arena.

This deep and delicate issue of a legacy of racism and its impact must be tackled within the treatment, therapeutic, or rehabilitative mindset with hired minority personnel primarily and/or trained and experienced personnel who truly understand racism real and perceived and/or those that have navigated a successful journey through racism. Quality culturally, competent personnel and treatment modalities must address the following:

- Assuring culturally competent staffing patterns
- the legacy of chemical dependency and the drug culture,
- the history and continual linkage of generational involvement in the criminal justice system,
- how to address the identity crisis among at-risk minorities, historical trauma, and post-traumatic slave syndrome
- the "victim to victor" transition,
- the act of assimilation or acclimation,
- racial identity development, exposing the positivity of one's legacy and future
- juvenile and young adult inpatient, outpatient, reentry, and diversionary programming to address the cultural identity crisis.

This is where "the conversation" can authentically demonstrate itself in a panoramic and fruitful display, planting the seeds of inclusivity, diversity, and understanding. Previously, I mentioned the past juvenile diversion program I ran, which was shut down by the corrections program I worked with. To be fair, those professionals are competent and qualified folks, but in my opinion, they were fearful of "the conversation." And as it's easy to do, they used the common phraseology and ideals of "evidence-based practices" and "strength-based" programming to hide the unknown fear of dealing with an issue that is entangled every day on multiple levels. While noble in their intent via the long-range scheme of things it is very heartbreaking for the cause of disparities that they failed to have "the conversation" that they themselves would say they embraced at the time. As we know, even amid these exceptional professional organizations and consequent policies, incarceration and collateral consequences continue.

A radical thought: In 2023, while working at a national training via the National Association of Public Defense's (NAPD) Racial Justice Conference in Alabama, one of the main features of this annual conference was to attend the transformative museums brought about by the work of the great, Bryan Stevenson. Those museums featured in this conference were *The Legacy Museum: from Enslavement to Mass Incarceration and the National Memorial for Peace and Justice*. Simply, these museums and many like them are astonishing. Referring back to the *Hidden Figures* movie where I didn't hear of that story until my forties, and while at this movie, to some degree, while personally knowing of slavery and its many impacts on my culture and while studying and researching aspects of it, these museums are on a whole other level. Words cannot describe them, but suffice it to say they bring you into the slave experience and its intertwined place in America. It also shows you the horrific onslaught of racist lynchings that took place throughout America. For those within the criminal defense community, not only do I suggest you attend the NAPD's Racial Justice Conference, but outside that, everyone should attend one of these museums, and specifically every African American!

My conjecture is, fully taking in the amazing creation of these museums in Alabama, as an African American, you cannot come from that experience not motivated to live a life fully and to the best of your ability, to live forward what many of our ancestors died for. There's a Juneteenth shirt I bought recently that better notes this sentiment. It reads on the front, "Dear Ancestors, I understand the assignment." That is the impact of this conference and the museums it features. More profoundly, the great Maya Angelou captures this sentiment impeccably. She writes in the infamous "Still, I Rise" poem,

> Leaving behind nights of terror and fear
> I rise
> Into a daybreak that's wondrously clear
> I rise
> Bringing the gifts that my ancestors gave,
> I am the dream and the hope of the slave.
> I rise
> I rise
> I rise.[78]

This is the meaning of legacy and making sure that it has a place in the American criminal justice experience. No detainee, offender, inmate, prisoner, probationer, parolee, or client of African American descent or one that gets a full grasp of the legacy of their heritage can settle to be a disparity statistic. Understanding the legacy of heritage is a powerful thing, and in our contemporary America, with most things at our disposal with a swipe of a finger on a smart phone or depending on the growing AI to do it for us, this principle shines even more true. This is not to say that criminal justice reform ends on all the frontend things it needs to continue to change, fight the power, and continue to, but it is to say, despite those continued and unfortunate realities, action toward change inside the system is just as needed. That is telling true story of how incarceration has been a vehicle of racism and even still, even in the face of torture, terrorism and death African American's, not to mention other cultures, stood tall so that those to come might have a better future.

With this powerful depth of culture and history the radical thought our question being, what if every detainee, offender, inmate, prisoner, probationer, parolee, or client within the control of the criminal justice system was required to attend these museums in person? How about virtually, as many would think me crazy to take these folks outside a lock and key to a museum? But is the previous so far-fetched...I would suggest current disparities and being content with such is farfetched. But as to the principle, if these museums, the work of Bryan Stevenson, and many others was able to penetrate courtrooms, jails, prisons, probation offices, parole boards, and offices of policy and program makers, it would bring about an inward identity tsunami where young minority men, women, and youth would not be satisfied with the conditions of the criminal justice system and all its horrible collateral consequences. It would induce a pride of self and culture that spurs a life of power, production, and yes, for those concerned about public safety, yes, lower recidivism and safe streets.

Exposure

A journey beyond disparities and the cultural identity crisis must involve efforts toward exposure, not only exposing clients to the positivity of their heritage, but a consequent encouraging identity and various initiatives that take clients out of their box and expose them to different people, places, and things. This also includes the goal to embolden a collective identity with all of humanity and the American ideal of "we the people." This is the more tactile piece of my philosophy, actually involving meetings, trips, and events to open the minds of clients to a world forbidden, hidden, or forgotten about for those that are less fortunate; yes, and sometimes intentionally so, to keep subcultures and majority cultures solvent.

The foundation quote of *The Pact*, the powerful documentary of Drs. Sampson Davis, Rameck Hunt, and George Jenkins overcoming their inner-city environment to all become doctors, symbolizes the focus on exposure:

> Our children cannot aspire to be what they cannot see.[79]

In my work on this thought of a cultural identity crisis, there has been no greater contemporary example of this idea from start to finish other than the stories of Drs. Sampson Davis, Rameck Hunt, and George Jenkins. An "if nothing else, get this" comment here, get ahold of their work, story, and book. It embodies not only the idea of exposure but also deep meaning that criminal justice systems should adopt.

In many respects, I could professionally sum up my opinion on the plight of criminal justice disparities and its solution with this point alone beyond the current hallmarks of criminal justice reform or the notions, theories, or think tank conclusions. It's not profound and complicated. In fact, hastily concluded, having never felt the scourge of physical slavery or racial oppression, in my opinion, this is essentially the most influential place where racism has won its battle. If I or anyone else identifies with crime or its various sociological partners, prosocial behavioral change will not occur no matter what evidence-based practice is used or punitive measure. As stated in various ways and consistently among at-risk minorities in the criminal justice system, there is an identification with normality of criminality, and to counter act that those within the criminal justice walls must be exposed to a prosocial identity with their culture and additionally what that means in a positive and practical American context.

As I spoke to various examples in my work, many of my clients have seen nothing but the criminal justice system and its various collateral consequences throughout their lives. It is their normality and, in my opinion, why they often do not leave that unfortunate cycle of life. Even when exposed to alternatives without heavy work to explain and retrain identity, they do not choose what seems to be a better alternative.

This is hard work, but the criminal justice system should be inundated with exposure to the many minority men and women who have shaped America. They must see minority judges, police officers, public defenders, and many others within other fields to understand what it truly means to be a person of their heritage. Every day, they should be exposed to people, professionals, events, classes, trips as mentioned previously and so on to understand that criminality and the criminal justice system aren't a part of their culture. This hits right where it counts, meaning when clients enter the courtroom, they shouldn't be the only minorities in the courtroom. The totality of the criminal justice system and beyond need to be culturally competent in philosophy and in within all its staffing patterns.

A radical thought: every state and federal jail, prison, corrections agency, and innovative law enforcement program or court program and public defender office must be mandated not only to expose cultural competency in their philosophy, practice, and programming but also orchestrate meetings, presentations, field trips and events that bring or expose professionals, professions and views from various walks of life that can relate to their clientele and their futures.

The criminal justice system must also be mandated to be culturally competent in its staffing patterns, meaning its staff needs to reflect the diversity of its clientele. This is a tough one for various reasons that cannot be facilitated here, but it is clear particularly post-Floyd 2020 that the business world has gotten this message. However, as I've seen and spoken to in this dialogue, the criminal justice system finds this a hard one to attend to…again too much to discuss and debate here, but this is a "put your money where your mouth is" equation particularly for those many criminal justice organizations, including public defender offices, that speak to all that is this dialogue and support cultural competency but somehow choose to not reflect it in their staffing patterns.

Opportunity

One of the functions I do to make sure I do my job well is to visit jails, prisons, and treatment programs so that I can properly know and recommend them to the court. In Arizona, Minnesota, and Colorado, I've had the privilege of visiting many. One tour I had with other mitigation specialist colleagues was in a Minnesota prison that featured a full barbering program in the mid-2000s (pre-Floyd). It was an amazing program for those who liked the trade and had plans of using that trade once they left prison. However, when asked if the clients received their barbering license once they completed this thorough and competent program, it was told us that they received everything up until that license and that they had to go through the rigors of getting that license once they were released from prison. That knowledge was very dissatisfying to many of us on that prison tour, realizing that it fell short of equipping those clients with the ability to be employed when they left and the fact that they had to go through various loops to be licensed as barbers once they left.

There's an old scripture that reads, "Hope deferred makes the heart sick, but a longing fulfilled is a tree of life."[80] As I have researched and learned the journey of my African American culture and many other journeys that are similar, there are critical junctures in the journey when things had an opportunity to go well but also very badly. This is often where "hope was deferred" and the latter became the reality. It could be explained via Fannie Lou Hamer's "sick and tired of being sick and tired" or through Dr. King's exclaim, "be true to what you said on paper!" This energy, if you will, was felt when we heard that the detainees could obtain everything but the barbering license. This, especially when understanding the major obstacles these detainees had to get their license once out of prison.

Moreover, my conjecture of a cultural identity crisis in the criminal justice system and proposing that academics, belief systems, legacy, and exposure would help thwart the disparity issues not to mention all of the various efforts, policies, new theories, reframing of mission/visions statements, various programs, and movements I've seen, heard and participated in my twenty-five-plus years of working in the criminal justice system (long breath); all of it means nothing if there is not opportunity for criminal justice clientele. For those in this business for a considerable amount of time, we have heard it all, seen it all, and yet see disparities exist and then the constant up and down rambling about crime in urban areas and frankly entrenched in minority communities. Simply, if true to our craft and throughout the criminal justice system, it is time to turn the corner on this issue, and if not, we will continue to break down the fire for prosocial behavior and hope.

This idea is more toward the reentry discussion, but it speaks a philosophy throughout the criminal justice system. Many would suggest that the disparity of minorities in the criminal justice system is equated to a lack of opportunity in America. Whether it's economics, red-lining, education, inappropriate laws and policing, historic racist policies, and on and on…lack of opportunity has created subcultures in America. And those subcultures typically statistically overrun the criminal justice system.

While the criminal justice system must hold individuals accountable, it must also be a place of opportunity once those individuals have been held accountable. The idea of "corrections" must really mean correcting. The idea of "rehabilitation" must really mean rehabilitating. The idea of behavioral modification must really mean changing behaviors. All this is linked to opportunity, or the opportunity that was denied to most individuals who come into the criminal justice system. Jails, prisons, courtrooms, and the totality of the criminal justice system must be about opportunity if it is to be a system that fights for public safety, behavioral change, holding people accountable, and, to this book's point, lowering minority disproportionality in prisons. While holding people accountable, there must be an adjacent strength-based component that leads to true opportunity. This would radicalize the criminal justice system and the fact of continual recidivism that truly hurts public safety more than you will ever hear in a courtroom or from the sensational news or the latest politician pushing a platform of "tough on crime."

To this point, in the mid-2020s (post-Floyd), I visited again a prison in Minnesota, to which they again showed us the barbering program. At this point, I had not worked in the Minnesota area for some years, and naturally, I wanted to probe this licensing issue I asked about years before. So, I asked "can inmates get their license while in prison," it was then answered yes, now they can. They can be fully licensed as barbers before they leave prison. This is opportunity. As previously mentioned prior to the work of the Second Chance Pell Experiment Initiative, which started under the Obama Administration in 2015 and gained strength in every administration after his initial work, prisoners could not get Pell Grants to take college courses. In 2020, it was lifted and fully recognized in 2023. This is opportunity.

The Floyd 2020 moment and many historical moments like it could be described by the fact that in 2020—yes, 2020—the violence of cops against black men strongly existed, and thus, it produced a collective outrage as we all saw it and the reactions to it. It brought about this sense of a "hope deferred" or another cultural halt at a place where we thought there was a new and blossoming opportunity. Internationally, it seems the world was "sick and tired," and that "hope was deferred" because, yet again, and with astonishing surprise, America was not being true to what it said on paper.

This hopelessness is a part of this cultural identity crisis. It aligns with a lack of opportunity and can lead to depression, a resultant lack of will to succeed, and fertile ground where criminality can be fostered because of no hope. This reality was brought out in the infamous Kerner Commission Report of 1968 by the then-President Lyndon B. Johnson administration. This report was a hallmark and seminal scholarly standard for race in America and codified that a lack of opportunity solidified by the racist conditions and resultant poverty fosters a lack of hope and consequent crime. Given the powerful conditions of its turbulent time, this was the unfortunate story of America and at a national level this report exposed a massive "elephant in the room". Sadly, the research and conclusions of this timely report speak forward to many at-risk minorities that frequent the criminal justice system today.

It is obvious that many minorities and further most detainees have been victims of a lack of opportunity in one shape or form. While this isn't an excuse for crime it explains it in great detail and gives a map to deter crime, or better its understanding to build proactive and promising solutions to crime. When coupled with the racialized context of America, its clutches are even more powerful and cyclical. The American criminal justice system must become an entity of opportunity as much as it is and should be an entity of corrective action. This alone would have a major impact on this notion of a cultural identity crisis and disparities in the criminal justice system.

A radical thought: It is mandated that in every jail, prison, or juvenile treatment program that, every punitive measure or sanction must be met with an adjacent or overall strength-based component that leads to true opportunity outside of behavioral modification efforts. Radically, when the probation officer submits their presentencing investigation report, that report also entails a plan of opportunity. How about when a court issues a sentencing for a client? It also issues a mandatory "opportunity" agenda that will give the convicted leverage to gain an education, vocational skills, and other societal anchors necessary to live outside prison.

The Unthinkable Meets Radical

As shown, there are various practical methods, foundations, and real-life efforts in place to give context to how to address disparities inside out. As it relates to practical methods that understand and focus on this notion of identity or culture, the previous examples and the majority of my research have shown that counseling and social service fields have also been sensitive to this synopsis and have developed competencies around this theory. Ethnic awareness and multi-cultural counseling have grown in popularity in local and state government agencies in the past decades. However, corrections competencies as they relate to the cultural identity crisis have appeared to be minimal and distant when it comes to rehabilitation, treatment, and lowering disparity.

If the criminal justice system is going to take on this issue of disproportionality of minorities in the criminal justice system, there must be a solidified, quantified, and policy-oriented commitment to dealing with this issue. This would mean going beyond knowing and researching the fact that the system has been racist and that there needs to be continued change. It would further mean understanding after centuries of the criminal justice system being used to incarcerate disproportionate amounts of minorities and the consequent effects of house that impacts a culture. There needs to be a purposeful approach to reaching deeper elements in its efforts to treat and rehabilitate, such as this cultural identity crisis. Purposeful policy, practices, and follow through in dealing with disproportionality and the cultural element would result in dealing with difficult issues and making tough decisions, but ultimately, it would lead to purposeful and intentional policies that make a difference with the issue. Ideally, it would result in lowering the amounts of minorities in the criminal justice system.

Understandably, there are other examples of organizations that work on these issues in our nation. This is a diminutive sampling and outcomes of what I've seen and reviewed in my practices, but they serve as examples of what I'm alluding to in regard to the culture/disparity issue, and they serve as examples that could be in every state in America. These examples are a few practical displays of how focusing on the cultural identity crisis can flesh itself out in making a difference for change with this dynamic and the continual issue of vast amounts of at-risk minorities in the criminal justice system.

When you stop and think about it, truly stop and think about disparities in the criminal justice system; it is truly unthinkable. Just as unthinkable as what happened to George Floyd in 2020, so, too, from a holistic view, are the greater implications of the total criminal justice system and what it means for minorities. Floyd is an example of many others who have died and who are in prison currently. Police violence is only one end of the disparity spectrum of criminal justice. This issue is historic, this issue is truncated, this issue is intentional, and this issue is stubborn. A radical but competent departure from the current ideals and philosophies that run the criminal justice system is needed if disparities are ever to discontinue. This doesn't mean abolishing the criminal justice system, but it does mean there needs to be a radically different one. In my professional opinion, academics, belief systems, legacy, exposure, and opportunity are radical philosophical or value-based foundations/objectives to build a newer criminal justice system and to change the disparities issues in the criminal justice system. I believe these components should be at the bedrock of every philosophy, program, and policy that guides the criminal justice system.

CHAPTER 10

Imperative Takeaways for Evolution Keepin' It Real

In March 2013, I was privileged to experience one of the most regal events in my professional experience in criminal justice work. It was the judge investiture of the chief of my district public defender office. This event featured many attorneys, the media, community leaders, and family and friends of the soon-to-be judge. It was certainly a gathering of some of the best of the best, and this was appropriately highlighted by the procession of district judges in symbolic representation of the Bench and in support of a newly crowned member. Having had the opportunity to attend other investitures, this was my first opportunity, and it was an eye-full and, for me, awe-inspiring.

As great as this event was personally for my former boss and those who admired her, and as awesome as it was to be around many great people I admire, I couldn't help noticing as it relates to the many professionals and attorneys at this event, that I was the only African American present along with very other few minority professionals. While there was no slight to this amazing event and the brilliant woman who was sworn in as Judge, it was a practical panorama of the local legal field and leadership in the southeast Minnesota region. Also, it was an example of a significant dearth of cultural diversity and a need to embrace diversity in law practice, especially in lieu of the high percentage of minorities these professionals must serve within criminal justice.

Elated for my former boss and another opportunity to be among great local criminal justice power brokers people, many great minds. I can't explain to you the illness I felt in my stomach. These many attorneys, law enforcement officials, political officials, department heads, and the like had no cultural similarities with many of the clients they worked with. As said, this was the first of various amazing and heartwarming opportunities that I've been able to sit in and see former colleagues become judges, not to mention various other events, committees, meetings, collective criminal justice efforts, and community endeavors, and resoundingly very few leaders and key staff members were the minority.

It is a great experience, but it is sobering when you consider that many who run the American criminal justice system often, not always, but often do not look like the people they over see in the criminal justice system. More importantly, as this is a controversial situation to navigate, the larger issue is, while at least many are amazing with the individuals I have been able to work with, it is often difficult for them to relate to the culturally competent mindset needed for work in the criminal justice system. Simply when you have diverse leadership and competent leadership that reflects the clientele served, there is a sensitivity, focus, and understanding of the issues of that clientele and consequently desired outcomes are better reached. In this context, we are talking about public safety, lowering recidivism, behavioral modification, and assisting in changing lives historically, which are certainly worthy of diverse leadership. This is not about affirmative action in the sense of equal hiring but about cultural competency, with the many things that have been discussed to this point. It is important to have cultural diversity in leadership to understand and tackle this issue of a cultural identity crisis. It is important to have diverse leaders and staff to brainstorm, assess, problem-solve, create, and review what is best for a criminal justice system that is overrun with black and brown clientele.

Cultural competency in staffing and leadership is one of many things to consider when addressing this very hard issue of a cultural identity crisis and lowering disparities in the criminal justice system. It is one thing to research, speak to, and support this ideology, but it's another thing to actualize it. Of all things, this is the proverbial "elephant in the room" that hardly gets competently addressed. How is it that those in leadership and key areas of staffing in the criminal justice system often do not look like those it represents and is mandated to oversee? More profoundly, how is it that this continues to be the norm?

One area where this elephant is clearly seen is from the client's perspective. Kenneth Troccoli brings this out impeccably in his article, "I Want a Black Lawyer to Represent Me: Addressing a Black Defendant's Concerns with Being Assigned a White Court." At the top of the article, he brilliantly describes a scenario that criminal justice professionals see every day, and for those who have done the work for even a small amount of time have heard it in one shape or form. He writes,

> "I want a Black lawyer to represent me." These are the first words you hear after you introduce yourself to your new client. You have been appointed to represent this man on a criminal charge. You are white. He is Black. You answer that you are an experienced criminal lawyer and will represent him to the best of your ability, regardless of his or your race. He responds that he too is experienced with the criminal justice system-a system that targets Black men, like himself, for prosecution far more than whites, that sentences Black men to prison more frequently and for a longer duration than whites, and that fails to acknowledge or address the role that race and racism play in the development, enforcement, and execution of the criminal laws established by "the system." You explain that the law does not allow the client, as an indigent, to choose his own lawyer. 'You can hire whomever you want to handle your case," you say, "if you have the financial ability to do so. Otherwise, the

> court chooses your lawyer for you, and there is little you can do about it, other than to decide to represent yourself."
>
> Your client is not satisfied with this response. He explains that an African-American lawyer will be better able to understand and appreciate the circumstances that resulted in the bringing of these charges and that he, the client, can trust a Black lawyer more than a white one. You agree that trust is indispensable to an effective attorney-client relationship, but you disagree that trust is unobtainable merely because you are white, and that you, as a white lawyer, cannot be as effective as a lawyer who is African-American. Sensing that you and your client have reached an impasse, you suggest that both of you give this matter more thought and discuss it further at your next meeting. Your client assents and you leave.[81]

This elephant is something my public defender colleagues experience over and over again daily. And while it may not come off as eloquently as Troccoli wrote, it is said by word and body language many times a day and throughout America. To extrapolate what this piece denotes is to unpack various things that are too much to write about in this discourse. But I challenge you to think about the historical and stubborn disparities we have reviewed over and over again and then ask why the issue still persists at unthinkable levels. Not to get away from the thought of a cultural identity crisis and its various implications, not to get away from the minority issue and the horrible collateral consequences, but could it be that the reason why this problem is so prevalent, in my view, is because we simply do not have cultural competent leaders and staff leading the criminal justice system's across America and consequently the knowledge base needed to bring about true criminal justice reform on said issues just is absent, and in many cases intentionally made to be absent. This "elephant in the room" topic and others come to mind if the criminal justice system is to tackle the idea of a cultural identity crisis and, more broadly, build a foundation to change the disparity dilemma.

Self-Preservation

When I raise this issue among professionals invariably, I always get the question, Why is there a need for minority leadership in criminal justice circles? Can't Euro-Americans or those without the primary race of clients in the criminal justice system do just as good of a job leading in the area of disparities as African Americans or other minorities can? The obvious mathematic or scientific answer would be an absolute yes, in my professional opinion. But I could use that same logic to conclude because there is more Euro-American leadership and important staffing positions in the criminal justice field, disparities of minorities in jails, prisons, and probation disparities continue to be a rampant problem. Simply, there is a lack of diverse thought on these issues, and the obvious is that current efforts to this point have failed this issue.

Certainly, I will not make that total leap because various leaders I know outside my race possess the care and competence to lead with this issue. But I will say at the end of the day, or I should invoke in my experience, human nature has the tendency to self-preserve. I don't say this negatively as much as it's a natural tendency to first take care of self, home, me and mine, my family, my people, and my culture. Second, it invokes one's worldview, and if there is a lack of diverse worldviews, the singular worldview rules. Because of that, it is my opinion, particularly in the criminal justice field, that it is imperative to have diverse leadership, and it should be mandated, yes mandated, in every state or federal organization that deals with high disparities to have diverse leadership and key staffing positions. I say that in the thought of this issue of a cultural identity crisis and how mandated leadership will augment particularly the goals of courts, jails, probation, and corrections to be more culturally competent.

Not to plug politics, but to use what I would consider is America's largest example of why this is important, the presidency of

Barack Obama stands as powerful proof. Regardless of whether you or I like his politics, he proved that diversity is critical. As a man of African American and Euro-American descent during Obama's presidency, he talked about and addressed issues of race like no president before him. He pushed issues along those lines and hired competent individuals who reflected diversity and believed in diversity. His presidential cabinet reflected his diversity values, and consequently, his presidency also had a passion for the issues of a diverse America. Consequently, many areas that didn't get the same attention before his presidency were addressed, among those the very issue of criminal justice reform.

Not completely concluded for sure, but in many ways, it's almost as easy, as mentioned before, as a mathematical equation, in that if you hire diverse leadership and staff, and they are competent, dedicated, and talented while being empowered to do their work, the outcome is natural that they will address issues of diversity and while tending to the needs of the majority. This is said by leaning on the argument that if you take care of America's minority cultures, you automatically will take care of America's majority cultures.

President Obama spoke on the Travon Martin/Black Lives Matter, convened a meeting with Dr. Henry Louis Gates Jr. and Sgt. James Crowley about the arrest incident, starting the Our Brothers Keeper Initiative, began the Second Chance Pell Experiment, and gave a resounding and historic speech on race before winning the presidency, 2008's "A More Perfect Union." He embodied issues of his heritage, which included both black and white. And to the point of this book, he became the first president to tour a United States prison in lieu of his passion for criminal justice reform, and then, in fact, he kicked off the idea of modern criminal justice reform that still continues to evolve and modify today. And to the point above, about assisting the majority when thinking of the minority, he started Obamacare. Sure, it's a lightning rod issue that all don't agree on. But as the pandemic of 2020 showed, racial disparities in health care are almost as bad as it is with the criminal justice system, showing health care isn't healthy, if you will, in black and brown American cultures. Hence, I'm sure one reason is that President Obama focused on better health care for all in America. This is a small list of what he and First Lady Michelle Obama and his family did directly or indirectly for the issue of diversity. Time doesn't permit to speak all that Michelle Obama did, but it is just as historic.

Now this is not a President Obama and Michelle Obama party truly. They are used to the greatest example of what it means to have a competent, diverse leadership. This is not to say that other Presidents were not concerned about issues of diversity; for instance, up until the presidency of George W. Bush, no president had assembled as diverse of a cabinet as he did. This is not to mention the great work he did in Africa that did not get much press.

The obvious question is, Would there have been as much of an emphasis on these issues if there was a Euro-American president in the Oval Office or better in our thought of criminal justice leadership and staffing? I cannot say for certain, but the historical evidence would prove to be the case that diverse leadership is critical for all. This is not an indictment on past Presidents because I can assure you that they themselves had issues close to their heart and to their identity that they were passionate about in office. This is the point why, and America knows this, why many were discouraged that Secretary Hillary Clinton did not get into presidential office in 2016. Yes, aside from the issues, aside from the titles Republican and Democrat, she would have brought women's issues to light that, to this point, have not been as important to the leadership landscape. It's just that simple and yet profound to balance meeting the needs of all. We saw this with the growing leadership of women in political leadership after Senator Clinton, as seen with Vice President Kamala Harris and many of the things she led. Like Hillary Clinton (and invoking a strength of the President Obama presidency) and understanding all the debate that stirred during and after Vice President Harris's historic presidential campaign of 2024 and how it was lost, many felt national discouragement that an American woman of African and Indian descent would not be able to bring her vast diversity and prowess to height of American leadership and power. Regardless of one's politics, she would have brought a wealth of diversity and needed perspective to America.

For those not of the democratic persuasion, I'm sure the previous examples were hard to swallow. I assure you they are mentioned only as an example. That example, cultural competency in staffing and leadership, is vital in regard to the concerns of this book. Self-preservation is great and a healthy holistic human prerequisite. It's the whole thing that the flight attendants speak to when they note, in case of an emergency, put your safety mask on first before you seek to help others. Simplicity, you can't help others if you are physically unable or dead…sorry to be so blunt. However, within a collective landscape, within a body or organization, the point is that leadership must be diverse to make sure all parties are represented. Otherwise, when there is no diversity amongst the power-brokers, leaders, and staff, those not represented often get left out.

An overridden criminal justice system with much diversity within its clientele (unfortunately) cannot afford to not have diversity in its leadership and staffing if the system wants a productive model that supports true criminal justice reform and meets the needs the 2020 change movement has called for. More specifically, going back to the culturally competent program I built and the county leadership that ended the programming, while sad it is completely understandable as their leadership was not diverse. There were all kinds of issues they had to consider as they did their "self-preserve," and at the end of the day, they could not stomach an African American program in their juvenile detention center. I contend that had they had diverse leadership, and as I would use this to speak to the totality of the criminal justice system, my program wouldn't have been at issue, and more to the point, minority disparities would not be a problem as it is still today in the criminal justice system.

Cultural Competency

To that end, cultural competency must become the rule of the day in criminal justice. I will repeat that cultural competency must be mandated throughout the criminal justice system. I've shown how cultural competency is a regular philosophy in arenas like social service or human services. Criminal justice must begin to not only own the philosophy but also ensure that culturally competent leadership and staffing are in place to see change and quality evolution. To use the voice of social work as an example, The National Association of Social Work (NASW), in the foundational document *Standards and Indicators for Cultural Competence in Social Work Practice*, developed a full lexicon on how cultural competence is to be exemplified in the social work practice. It stands as an example of what could and should mean in this context and within the criminal justice system. Of their various descriptions, they note this foundational definition of what it should mean,

> Cultural competence requires self-awareness, cultural humility, and the commitment to understanding and embracing culture as central to effective practice.[82]

Take away the references to social work and put them in the criminal justice system, law enforcement, the court system, probation agency, jails, prisons, district attorney's office, public defender office, and juvenile treatment program. To be fair, many service organizations and criminal justice departments have these same types of written ideals or goals. They show a written commitment to diversity. The problem is usually in the implementation, and additionally, in my opinion, diversity in leadership to ensure a passionate follow-through is nonexistent.

While there are many words and phrases that describe the diversity, equity, and inclusion (DEI) journey, and I will not be ignorant to understand that "cultural competency" is an older phrase that is not as cool or welcomed as the latest verbiage on DEI, however for me, it hits to the point when it comes to professions that are required to work with minority cultures, in this case, the criminal justice system. The various other terms and phrases are valid and, in many cases, nullify the use of this term, but again, when it comes to all professions within the criminal justice system, my conjecture is that this term is the best to use. "Cultural" speaks to culture (previously defined and spoken to in the DSM-5-TR referencing. On that obvious foundation, the key part for me is the word "competent." Competency is something that is a requirement when it comes to one's profession, trade, or organization. It's often those baseline requirements to be licensed, viable, and productive. Note the NASW definition again and note the words "requires," "commitment," and then the term "central to effective practice." These terms exude additional words like mandatory and imperative.

For instance, as a licensed social worker, I must meet certain competencies to be licensed, viable, and productive, with cultural competence being one of them. Without those competencies in place, I cannot be a social worker. My reference to cultural competence speaks to mandated portfolio within the criminal justice system to be licensed, viable, and productive. This includes the totality of the system: police officers, prosecuting attorneys to defense attorneys, correctional officers to judges, treatment programs to behavioral modification/corrective efforts, juvenile detention facilities to jails, prisons, and probation/parole caseloads.

Given all I have spoken to refer to this cultural identity crisis, there is no leverage to balance a criminal justice system in any current form without cultural competency. On the statistics of criminal justice disparities alone, without theories that speak to its reality, cultural competence is still "mandatory" and "imperative."

Treatment Foundations

What I sought to do through most of this book is to provide a basis for an emphasis on corrective and treatment efforts in focus on a cultural identity crisis. Whether it's my thought of a cultural identity crisis or other researched concepts on which it stands, the soul would, historical trauma, post-traumatic slave syndrome, racial identity development, ethnic-racial identity development, or other aspects or theories that some associate with this dynamic, the idea is these ideas must be at the foundation within criminal justice.

I have made my case as to why I believe it's along the lines of a cultural identity crisis, but for the sake of argument, if it were some of the other elements, we must begin to conclude how disparities historically began, how they, unfortunately, continue via the dynamics raised from the great work of Michelle Alexander and others... these areas are not the only culprit of disparities. The War on Drugs, improper policies, historical racism, horrible court decisions, overreaching sanctions on felons post-prison, and on and on are important and are anchors in the journey, but we must begin to figure out a plan to help a culture of people that since this nation's beginning have had a relationship with criminal justice that is history unhealthy to place where many equate criminality with normality. Or to a place where the residuals of incarceration have been so impactful it sometimes seems impossible to change course for generations.

Corrective and treatment programming in prisons, jails, courts, and probation caseloads must begin with the foundations of many of the concepts I've mentioned in this book. Across the board and per state and federal policy, culture competency, and diverse leadership must be the rule of the day when dealing with many at-risk populations that frequent the criminal justice system.

It's as simple as the old adage: you can give a man a fish, or you can teach him to fish. Both are noble, but one will lead to continual bondage. Advocacy and activism for criminal justice reform on front-end issues alone (Black Lives Matter, drug law change, sentencing, policing) is almost akin to giving fish to at-risk men, women, and juveniles that have been so damaged with the collective collateral consequences of historic imprisonment that a mere change in plight will not change them going back into criminal justice bondage. However, these noble and needed ventures, coupled with corrective and treatment focus in and out of prison, will lend to a complete empowerment that allows these same at-risk cultures and generations forward to find their way out of some of racism's most profound and multi-layered clutches, negative identity and residual behavior. The battle for why black and brown lives get into jails and prisons needs to continue, but it must as enthusiastically be battled in the "justice," "corrections," and "rehabilitative" ideals of courts, jails, and prisons.

The Conversation or Legislation

One of the things I consistently hear in my work, both in the system and areas of community advocacy, and I really admire it if it can happen, is this constant cry for America to have "the conversation" about race. Truly, in its most therapeutic sense, it would help the healing in this nation. But such a discussion and actual discussion that is going forward need to embody honesty and residual action. "The conversation" without action is merely church without going outside of the church to feed the hungry sitting outside of the church building.

The truth is power-brokers are going to have a really hard time with making necessary policies and actions that deal with what "the conversation" reveals. Let alone the power-brokers and everyday people don't want to discuss it anyways. Whether it's disguised in the "color blind" notion that we say we are living in or hope we will live in or totally ignoring history altogether, it's hard for everyday people to really talk about race. No matter your position on the theory, issues around the subject, like the critical race theory in schools, prove it's hard to have that conversation.

This goes for the criminal justice system as well. No one wants to hear this noise about a cultural identity crisis in jails and prisons and many issues around race. It hits on too many real issues and, in many cases, doesn't help the bottom line. Yep, I said that. Many would rather wrap up these issues in "you do the crime, you do the time" and/or be content to be in the choir cheering for change and then clocking out at 5:00 p.m. and going home to my safe community with no diversity.

This goes for people within the historical oppressive culture and those in the historical oppressed cultures. Yes, my African American culture doesn't get a pass to own its part—absolutely not. Huge, but there are some things we need to own, definitely in our contemporary capitalistic society. But all in all, to get the average American to really talk about race in a way that leads to life-changing outcomes is "not gonna happen" on average. Some of this is due to human nature, guilt, confusion, or a flat-out denial and a whole lot of immaturity.

But for whatever reason, it's likely not to happen as it's advertised in its fashionable and cool-sounding ways.

The truth is if I don't want to talk about it, I don't, especially if my "self-preservation" is working really well. That is the truth about anyone, and we are wrong if we, even if fashionable, get dismayed at those who will not talk about it. The backlash against DEI in the 2020s is a massive example of this. DEI is being rejected, and I'm not saying that during this time, that was a good idea, but it points to no one wanting to get real about this and have the conversation.

However, and a big however, as a collective society and given the vast negative consequences of racism and, in this context, the criminal justice system, human nature must be outmaneuvered by law and policy. While the conversation is too tough to have, legislation must get above human tendency. Law is put into place many times because we know what human nature, in its average sense, will do or not do. The truth is that neither this book nor will any conversation change historical racism in the criminal justice system. But law on top of it will.

We saw this with slavery in the 1800s and the need for the passage of law outlawing slavery, and in the 1900s, with the need for the passage of civil rights law. "The Conversation" is great, not to mention those that accompany American streets to rally for social change, but this will not see anything done unless legislation is in place. The work of Michelle Alexander and others, the awesome Netflix documentary *13th*, and other works, yours truly, and what I've humbly tried to add to the effort is nothing if "The Conversation" doesn't become legislation.

While writing this book, at one point, I was watching MSNBC's *Morning Joe*, a past ritualistic favorite of mine, early mornings before work to watch various morning new outlets. World-renowned and former anchor, Tom Brokaw, was on the show talking about the unrest with many groups. In particular, he was referencing the protests in Berkley, California, in early 2017. He mentioned a quote that I had never heard, and I thought it was magnificently profound for what he was addressing. He noted as if he was a mentor to all that rallied in Berkley incidents and forwarded a message to all that march for social change, "rage is not a policy." The civil rights era America proved that protests, marches, and MLK's quote, "Riot is the language of the oppressed," pushed for true change. But all those things are nothing unless laws are passed as a next step. In like fashion, as noble and cool as "the conversation" can be and as productive as it can begin, it means nothing if it's metamorphized into policy.

The conversation of this book has been ruminated and researched in one shape or form. Different phrases and even different conjectures, but all leading to a need to focus on swiftly changing the plight of changing disparities in the criminal justice system. I hold myself accountable for these great conversations. What then are the next steps?

Where the Real Racism Exists

From Trayvon Martin to George Floyd and beyond, America in the mid and late 2020s saw racial incidents and atrocities that have been emblematic of the 1960s. It can be said that civil rights energy was equally the same. While things are obviously better with respect to overall racial history in America, racism still lives, and it seems that there are forces that want it to stay. What I've learned in my education on racism is that it is prejudice connected to power breeds the same in governance and society. Overt racism in word and deed is hurtful, overt racism at the end of a police officer's gun is diabolical, and overt racism in housing, education, and economics is horrific. However, I would suggest, and this conjecture on my part, that if you were to go with me to the various jails, courts, or prisons, I do for my vocation and if you worked in the various circles I do with various criminal justice professionals you would see where I think the exponential racism exists.

Going back to the previous "fish" analogy, it is my opinion that the criminal justice system currently has no intention of teaching the many at-risk minorities in their clutches to truly "fish." This is not a blanket statement on all criminal justice systems, but as a whole, it is failing. This could be overt in its power, indirect in its influence, or it could be the guilt that comes collectively about having "the conversation." But I can say through my study and local efforts that when seeking to delve deep to radically change behavior by empowering African Americans with the essence of their identity and the power of who they are and can be, this is met with resistance and certainly ignorance.

I would suggest the power of disparities and racism in the criminal justice system is not primarily at the wrongful arrest of a police officer or the court's punishment for behavior. It's in correctional and probation systems that are not built to teach cultures how to get out of criminal justice bonds and the collective collateral consequences that keep cultures in the criminal justice system. This is the epicenter of change, in my professional opinion: empowerment of the mind of one's true identity into action that does not normalize criminal behavior or justify it as the only way to survive. Upon that positive foundation, disparities can change, but if there is no change toward a mandated culturally competent American criminal justice process, America will continue to see the collective recidivism that has been historic and continually damaging to black and brown lives.

Reparations

Reparations are a constant thought among the African American community and have made it into mainstream debates. It is not something that is talked about much, but it still has an undercurrent and sometimes seems to be building steam. Reparations are an aspect where America should pay back African Americans and other oppressed cultures for slavery and the hard work that was never awarded through the arduous work of slaves. I'm not a fan of this idea because of its practicality of implementation, but the concept is understandable, and if it can be done equitably, it certainly has merit. I think it needs a different look to be practical and make sense. Controversial, but take a minute to follow me.

When it comes to the vicious historic leg of the criminal justice system on minorities, I do think there should be some kind of reparations. However, in this context, it is not a paying back in an economic way, as that would be too complicated. However, in response to the historic systems of oppression that have stood in the way of minority progress, there could be what I'd term reparations-lite. More specifically, in this context, it would be in a way that the federal and state criminal justice entities build therapeutic, treatment, reentry, and corrective and educational structures that change the plight of these historical disparities and their collateral consequences. It would include the current hallmarks of criminal justice reform and the holistic ideas championed in this book and via many other well-documented and decorated champions of criminal justice reform.

This idea goes toward my belief that stats like the "one in three African American men will enter the criminal justice system" is the strongest impact of racism because the collateral consequences of such cripples everything with regard to economics and the American Dream. For example, what if all prisons (all meaning some already do this, but it isn't consistent across America), while "keeping the public safe," also became the epicenter of remedial education but also post–secondary education and vocational skills to assist those that are willing to build opportunities to earn a decent living once out of prison. This would mean even going beyond the Pell Grant opening to allow education to be a free feature of prisons. What if prison was known to prepare the best of the best for today's workforce and college degrees once someone has served their time and showed a commitment to behavioral change?

What about the idea of expungement of a sentence? Many times, a criminal record is the principal barrier to getting into school or getting a good job. What about a federally mandated system in all states that is consistent and allows former felons to expunge their criminal records after a supportive but rigorous program that builds reentry, education, vocational skills, licensures, and college degrees while allowing for the focus on corrective, treatment and therapeutic needs? This further would be supported by competent, safe, and supportive housing. Meaning, every detainee or former detainee gets a free but rigorous path to not only build a career and get an education but also have housing and an expunging of their record once requirements are met. It goes without saying that some offenses and behaviors might be excluded, but by and large, a powerful reentry effort is mandated.

These ideas are but a few, and other ideas outside of the criminal justice system in the same vein would be a different and more plausible and practical look at what reparations could look like and what America can actually do. This is said to know the power of what incarceration has done to generations. Now with these types of ideas in mind, rethink the reparations conversation and what it might be able to really do. My nature is not quick to say anyone owes me or my culture anything. I will be bold enough to say that most of my African American culture would agree with this through the infamous quote, "We don't need a hand-out, we need a hand-up," and that within the criminal justice system. Reparation is a noble topic and practically understood. A modified focus on it could work toward its original intentions. In this context, America owes African Americans and other minorities through an immediate evolution in the criminal justice system to change the plight of disparities. What we have seen historically and currently in this regard is not American. Tackle the existence of historic disparities and its collateral consequences via the criminal justice system, it would meet a huge anchor of what reparations are calling for.

Keepin' It Real

In review, I want to be careful to note that punishment and corrective action are needed in any civilized country or culture. This book is not about not punishing people for crime and excusing crime. I do not like the word punishment, but it is what it is, and punitive measures are a needed necessity. Any thought along those lines would be completely and utterly untrue from the standpoint and premise of this book.

The goal of this book was to unearth a true idea on how to correct behavior and build positive futures within the criminal justice system's foundational ideals and embarrassing problems with disparities of black and brown lives in its systems. Criminal justice is not only about punishment as we know; it is about correcting behavior and supporting rehabilitation, hence the name "corrections," and now some departments like California have adopted the verbiage "corrections and rehabilitation," similarly, Arizona has adopted the name, the Arizona Department of Corrections, Rehabilitation, and Reentry. Another example is the mission statement of the Minnesota Department of Corrections, "Achieving justice through the promotion of racial equity, restoration from harm, and community connectedness." While seemingly radical and certainly "out of the box," these notions and goals of this book are about true public safety and lowering recidivism.

Additionally, it is about taking a look at criminal justice disparity against the backdrop of continual criminal justice-laden incidents and topics such as Black Lives Matter, police violence, unrest in urban cities, criminal justice reform, and true DEI and its need. Further challenges include asking these efforts and discussions about how to address these problems to look deeper into a more therapeutic and culturally competent bent. Principally concluding, the activism and advocacy fall short if it does not take into context the cultural identity crisis and well-documented topics of the soul: historical trauma, post-traumatic slave syndrome, racial identity development, and ethnic-racial identity.

Statistics easily show that if a society wants public safety, safe streets, and to calm the fear of crime, "tough on crime" efforts and just locking people up are not the answer. It is *not* the answer; it delays the inevitable, builds a larger climate for crime, and solidifies subcultures or an American caste system. The research and evidence are abundantly clear. When criminal justice systems work toward holistic and evidence-based efforts to change and support positive behavior, this is more supportive of everyone's desire for a safe and productive society. Leaning on the worlds of the late great Minnesota Senator, Paul Wellstone, "We all do better when we all do better." As to the 35 percent to 40 percent of African Americans and other minorities that are currently in jails and prisons, they need a culturally competent programming and support to assist them in not recidivating back to prison. This historic and sad issue needs to change to meet the moment of public safety and criminal justice reform.

PART 3

Closing Argument
A Call to Action

CHAPTER 11

The Acid Test
A Personal Reflection

Early January 2011 in Rochester, Minnesota, I found myself at a community meeting for the *ISIAIH* organization, a Minnesota group of faith congregations, clergy, and people of faith to act collectively and powerfully toward racial and economic equity in the state of Minnesota.[83] The organization was looking to launch in the southeast, and they had a focus on upgrading area practices and policies that addressed at-risk populations and crime. In my work, I'm often at various meetings or on board or committees seeking to find out-the-box methods to assist my clientele in sentencing proceedings. This was an introductory meeting for me and other community and others. As an icebreaker and to build commonality, the leader asked the group of area leaders to speak of their personal and professional journey and add aspects of opportunity or a lack of opportunity. Prior to beginning, the leader described his personal journey to his current life and profession. He then correlated his experiences to systemic problems in minority and at-risk populations in Minnesota and the United States. I later learned his goal of this initial exercise was to note the privilege or a lack of privilege he had in his life and what impact it had.

After he finished telling his story, he directed the group of twenty to twenty-five to split into smaller groups and tell their stories of journey and privilege. As I sat there, I thought I would hear similar stories to mine because we were all there to impact at-risk populations, and for sure, there would be many from the side of the tracks that we were seeking to assist with. Each person told their story in our group, and I found myself in a usual but unusual place, among these accomplished professionals and somehow in my psyche, wondering if I was more or less one of them. But as if it were a time-warped moment, I was definitely feeling these thoughts, "How in the world did I get here because I certainly didn't have the privilege and position that most of these people had?" and "What were the dynamics of my journey that assisted me in getting where I am and how can that be multiplied with those I work with daily?" While around many good-hearted and impactful southeast Minnesotans engaged in the battle to "make a difference," as always, I realized not many, comparatively, succeed out of the circumstances of the stereotypical at-risk minority upbringing. While there are many great stories of overcoming, there are many more that simply do not make it to American success. I managed to tell my story, but it was with an abbreviation because I was thinking about the deeper elements that even had me at the table with such amazing people.

In this business, the criminal justice business, and acutely as a public defender and certainly being a person who loves sports, the "rags to riches" stories it often highlights in this context these stories are very interesting to me. Such stories and similar ones in from many dynamics could be literal "rags to riches," poverty to an actual millionaire. Or they can be figurative rags to riches, one like in my case where someone might beat the streets, overt negatively, horrible life traumas and consequently the riches piece is that they manage to get a good education, job, and family or other hallmarks we relish to one that is successful. As we know, money does not guarantee one has made out of "the hood," the old adage, you can take a country boy out of the country, but you can't take the country out of the boy. Regardless, whether monetarily or holistically, this dynamic is a huge part of the American story, or we romantically want it to be. In some respects, that is my story, but while not highlighting "the hood" or the various tales of the "dysfunctional family," what grew from this initial question at the meeting grew into what this book is all about.

As an African American male, full of the upbringing stereotypes that would assure my future doom, how did I win the proverbial "success" lottery to escape my statistical-founded impending doom to become who I am today, Dr. Donavan Bailey, instead of inmate Donavan Bailey? Success can be defined in many ways, and respectfully, one can be successful in prison or out of prison. Success here is holistic. But assuredly, how did I escape some of the unfortunate realities of many young men who grew up in the same areas and with the same life dynamics but unfortunately succumbed to tragedies of what the "one in three" African American men speak to?

I was born into a typical Midwestern major city in an African American family that experienced the ups and downs of living city life with the residuals of racism. "Naptown," Indianapolis, was my birthplace and where I grew up as an at-risk youth. For a short time, just before the age of five, our family came to experience a life of the middle class living in what would be the suburbs of Indianapolis at that time, the Ben Davis area. But that was short-lived after my parents got a divorce. Soon, my father was completely out of the picture of my life. My mother, as typical to many single mothers, took on the role of two parents and simply could not afford to rear her three sons, the youngest of which was me, in the middle-class lifestyle. From there, I proceeded to live the journey of a Midwestern city and the inner-city lifestyle.

Certainly, I experienced some of the stereotypical and real situations of living in an urban major city. Those situations typically become media headliners for attraction and often become badges of honor for those who live in the hood and certainly for those who make it out of the hood. As is the motif of this book and understanding of these real dynamics, these descriptors of at-risk minority life and our identity with these descriptors are far outdated and, while very real, are overplayed. Further, there needs to be no extra description and attraction as it relates to my personal journey and those evident descriptors. Again, somehow, our "Reality TV" culture has fabricated those aspects into an overhype that many think is normal and most certainly entertaining. However, one aspect needs to be noted, and it is a consistent aspect that equates to most of those attractive descriptors. While there was the absence of positive male role models, poverty, crime, and drugs, in my opinion, more evident was this consistent issue of the real and perceived residuals of racism and its impact on my identity and how it impacted how I acted and reacted.

One interesting scenario that impacted how I act and react today is the convenience store experience. It's old school, but many can relate to this scenario. I have grown to understand that this could be a real or perceived issue, but from a standpoint of understanding, it is highlighting racism and its history. I can remember many times as a youth going to the local convenience store, getting the infamous milk, bread, and cereal for home or just going to get my favorite pack of $0.25 bubble gum. As I grew as a youth, there was not one time I went into the store that I didn't feel the store personnel either staring at me or following me through the store, thinking I was going to steal something. "It is was it is," or was what it was, but now even as an African American man, when I leave a convenience store without purchasing something, I struggle with the thought of "you will always be suspected as a thief in convenience stores, clarify often." I feel like I have to validate to the cashier before leaving that I didn't purchase anything or the fact that I'm not sure what I want, and that's why I'm in aisle 2, staring at which high-priced item I'm going to buy.

This odd and comparatively small example is emblematic of larger scenarios played out in African American culture. It, of course, has legitimate roots, and wherever it started. I allowed a bad experience or supplanted idea to become a part of my identity, and it caused me, in this case, minor anxiety when I go into convenience stores about who I was and how I had to act and react in this situation.

As an overall description, looking back, having grown and experienced other major American cities, my Midwestern city and inner-city experience can be described as a slow death, not literally of course. But while it had crime and many of the things stereotypically associated with a major city and urban stress, those things seem to be like a dark cloud over the city. And while not overt in ways of a Los Angeles or a New York City of its time (late 1980s), it seemed more like a terminal illness rather than the immediacy of violence and consequences often described in the media about urban cities.

As mentioned, the media will highlight the sensational, and perhaps most major cities can be described this way. While Indianapolis was not reeling with the complete domination of gang activity, race riots, over-stretched poverty, population explosion, and American anarchy, as the nation's thirteenth largest city at that time (sixteenth at the time of this book), its inner city life was an amalgamation of a wide range of various components and somewhat reactionary components to systemic racist practices of history and that day. This is not new to the American landscape, and for that reason, Indianapolis was like many cities. It was a decent city that lived with the scourge of racism. But this city, as it was to me and given the previously described dynamics, was again like that idea of a "slow death" within its inner-city climate, and one wished the systemic issues of racism, poverty, crime, drugs, and oppression would get over and become sensational because you lived with this day in and day out and a "quick death," if you will, seemed better than working and living with the tired consequences of racism.

While my mother worked hard and did her best to rear three young black men, my fate was statically etched as many at-risk African American youth. A foundation was set for me to not succeed or to have challenging "baggage" in my life that would challenge the grip of success when it was at my fingertips. However, at the age of thirteen, something happened, particularly as I gazed in the review mirror and tried to understand how I landed where I am in life, as opposed to the many who grew up in the same conditions but didn't make it out of the hood. Success is measured on many different levels, and to one person, success is one thing, and to another, it is a different thing. But in the atmosphere that I grew up in and around, somehow, I attained something akin to success in life that others had not, and as I look back and measure how that came about, it was a key component around the aspect of identity. Simply, through the mixing of several dynamics, I began to change my identity at the age of thirteen.

The teenage years are the key place for that aforementioned "identity crisis" (Eric Erickson) with various struggles and double-over, in my opinion, for an at-risk minority from a historically oppressed culture. The negative influences were there, but for reasons I will explain, I was able to not allow what I was seeing and experiencing to define me. I began to identify myself as something different than statistics predicted, what my environment provided for me, or what the racial struggle tried to make me to be. And this new identification, I would attest, wasn't this major goal to beat the odds and the front end of my evolution.

By no means am I the crowning view of American achievement, but I know that I would not have succeeded personally, professionally, academically, spiritually, and relationally without understanding my identity through these imperative dynamics that unfolded in my teenage experience. Simply amid the challenges that are often glorified, amid the sullen weight of urban life, amid the racism that was rampant in my upbringing, amid the challenges of any "normal" youth, I began to identify with key prosocial norms that if I was to put my life story of "rags to riches" on the Broadway marquee it would note the following as my key to success, "cultural identity evolution."

In surveying my personal life and answering the personal question of how I was able to grow away from the negative aspects or predictors for my life, the following are key areas of this proposed cultural identity evolution that led to me from the statistical norms of at-risk African American youth to living beyond what was the norm. The ideas are adjacent to dealing with this idea of a cultural identity crisis through the various theories previously used, and they found eventual success in positive ethnic-racial identity development. Further, these aspects are adjacent to my professional philosophy and were the anchors that tell the tale of how one, Dr. Donavan Bailey, was able to attain a life that even I had no clue I could attain. These anchors were previously mentioned: academics, belief systems, legacy, exposure, and opportunity. As previously mentioned, there are other journeys that can describe other imperative aspects. There are various competent and commendable stories of how individuals made it out of "the hood" or equally or even more aggressive harsh childhood and youth conditions. For me and my journey, these were critical. I have further concluded that for many of the at-risk minorities that inundate the criminal justice system, these components are likewise key to changing the plight of disparities in the criminal justice system. I again attest that these components should be a part of any corrective or treatment focus seeking to rehabilitate the lives of at-risk minorities in the criminal justice system. The following are how these were personally applicable and impactful to my personal success:

Academics

My formal and qualified education, in my opinion, did not start until I attended an area private school in Indianapolis during my junior year and senior in high school. Of course, I somehow (and truly hard to even think how I did) passed each grade prior to that in the public schools. I had some educational aptitude, but it was when I went to this demanding private school that educationally, things became extremely difficult and pushed me to an educational level that I couldn't comprehend at the time. While this time was more of an arduous journey that seemed to churn up an unfruitful educational ground, this education was of massive value to this at-risk African American young man. Prior to attending this institution, I can't remember much academically in my public education other than dissecting a cow in freshman biology class at Northwest High School.

Not only was I challenged academically, but my attitude and behavior were challenged. There was one incident in which I was almost expelled from school and went back to the failing public school. For me, this was a critical moment. For behavior, I cannot fully remember my aberrant "bad boy" who showed up one day in class, and frankly, at the time, I do remember thinking it was funny. I also remember it was my edgy mouth and lack of respect for authority that caused disruption in the class. For my behavior and completely warranted, I received a suspension from the school from the principal.

I was so angry about this situation because I thought my bad behavior would get me out of school for a week, and so at first, I thought it was no big deal, a vacation from school. But it landed me sitting in a room alone working on schoolwork for a week, in something this principal called an "in-school suspension," not a real suspension from school. It was very hilarious looking back, but in my at-risk mind, this was unacceptable, and I let the principal know about it. In fact, I told him I was going to serve my suspension out of school because that's how the public school did it. In so many frank words, Principal Thomas of now-named Crosspoint Christian Academy told me that if I left the school, I would not be coming back. I was ticked. I called my mother and ranted and raved, and she allowed this to be my decision. Whether by divine intervention or personal fear, I decided to serve that in-school suspension.

This was a pivotal moment for me because, in the passion of my at-risk mentality, I almost blew an opportunity that changed my life, and I could just as easily be lived by my distorted view of "keeping it real" and walked away from a significant anchor of my life. As I said, I only attended this private school for two years, my junior and senior years. But without those two years of private school education, I would not have been able to handle college life. Which then led to graduate school and a doctoral degree.

This experience, as well as other future experiences, grew my value for education and built an identity with education as a necessity. Among the many legitimate issues around education, for me, it revolved principally around identity and adopting this as a part of my personage. In my community, by consequence or acceptance, it was devalued. Education has somehow been devalued, and among the issues fostering the existence of an achievement gap is the fact that having a quality education has not been pushed to be authentic to African American identity. This statement is a broad-stroke statement that isn't true of every individual or necessarily of African American life. Many would successfully argue that it is the exact opposite. I stress it has been pushed to be and is consequent to racism. Moreover, the problem has been a culture of at-risk minds settling with this notion and the statistical realities of the achievement gap. Of course, I don't believe this is an abiding foundational characteristic of choice, and history will prove that in the quest to overcome racism, a loss of culture, and the bonds of slavery, denying a quality education was one of the main tools to keep African Americans in bondage. While not as overt, today's issues of the tale of a lack of education continue. However, education is a cornerstone of the African American identity and history, but you wouldn't know it if you looked at today's world.

Given African American's identity with education, it is almost unthinkable that somehow the notion of education not being positive crept into the African American experience and is seen as rare among competent professionals. It is obvious and too much to list here but from our notable HBCUs to countless historical and contemporary educators and education institutions, it is clear education was a vital and expansive part of African American life. Highlighted by the fact that the first African American and woman to be an American Vice President and presidential candidate was a graduate of an HBCU, Vice President Kamala Harris of Howard University. Not to mention President Barack Obama and Supreme Court Judge Ketanji Brown Jackson and their educational prowess.

Many who are reading this are probably laughing at me as I'm just scratching the surface of many national and local education champions, schools, leaders, and normal everyday Americans with high-level advanced degrees to technical education and careers. Indeed, laughter should ensue, and it is hilarious when you consider how too many at-risk minority lives have a twisted idea about their identity and it not being linked to education. It's unbelievable even in the professional world when rarity is linked with those who are African Americans or other minorities and who are educated. So much so the racial barriers to education aren't seen as the culprit but the idea that education isn't a part of the African American cultural identity.

In fact, the phrase "sell out," while coined for other reasons, sometimes was a word I fought when returning home from college to the area in which I grew up. At the time, because I was seeking an education, somehow, I was less than African American to many of my at-risk peers and culture. Even now, past POTUS Obama, it is still somehow odd for an African American man to be educated, and obviously, America is still dealing with disparities in education for African Americans and other minorities. There are various ways to challenge and overcome this national issue, some of which I described in the book apply not only to a failing criminal justice system but also to a failing education system.

However, what was important to me, amid the obstacles to getting an education and beating the stereotypes of what it meant to be educated as a black man, was when it became a part of my identity. Not having it was not an option. Through education, I came to understand that education was a vital and essential aspect for any person wanting to succeed, definitely for any at-risk minority to succeed. Accordingly, I realized that if I didn't receive a quality education and value that education, it is almost certain that my life would have likely devolved to crime and its effects. When I ended my education at that private school, it was embedded in my identity, my psychological DNA that I was going to college and beyond, and it became a habit.

Belief Systems

My belief system is another integral piece to my life as an at-risk African American child growing up in a major city. This also started and grew foundationally in my life around the age of thirteen. Particularly, this is key because, coming from the background that I did, I did not have many appropriate venues to foster my identity. In essence, I was empty of self, and at some point, I was going to find my belief system, worldview and/or spiritual foundation, whether positive or negative. While this could have come from the many negative avenues that were evident, gangs being a major stereotypical conclusion and, in my case, negative associations, I found faith and spirituality as a massive anchor to offset this idea of a cultural identity crisis, potential criminality and this helped build a positive foundation my life.

This anchor sets the soil for numerous amounts of prosocial perspectives, decisions, and overall life dynamics. This piece, for this empty, at-risk African American young man without form and foundation, gave immediate context for everything as a youth just prior to the various destructive influential aspects that began to influence my life. This was critical because the crime associated with most males in my family and deeply rooted in the at-risk culture within my family was not acceptable according to the new belief system I began to follow. Additionally, the negative portrayals of my culture and facets of racism, much more evident in that time in the media and throughout life, were not acceptable to be a part of my makeup nor influence aggression toward obvious racist sway from individuals and entities.

While not perfect by any means, I was able to escape many of the pressures associated with urban life. When I faced challenges and the average difficulties that most go through, this worldview assisted me with a proper perspective. When I had to look into myself and find something that I didn't see to succeed, it produced energy and motivation to continue. When I faced things that were unexplainable, and there was no earthy and positive answer for, it gave context. Yes, even when I felt that my America wasn't mine, a growing understanding of how racism hurt my people and me personally, it gave me a broader understanding of a greater humanity and a bigger worldview. Moreover, when religion was the culprit of madness, racism, vice, and oppression, yes, it gave solace. It was my faith ethic and principles, thereby that provided motion and a holistic mental complex to persevere in my purpose. It gave me an identity of self that explained my past, present, and future that no one or thing could take away.

As mentioned earlier, this aspect is controversial and hard to imagine implementing in the criminal justice system. Also, faith is an absolute scary thing, as Trump's presidency showed in America. It can go to levels of fanaticism, blind fellowship, and cultish behavior. That goes for any religion or over-entrenched belief in a person, system, theory or even country. However, building one's personal faith ethic, worldview, and spirituality whatever that might be, is crucial to any person, especially to lives grown up in at-risk and high-risk lives. I would attest that everyone has a core belief system, good, bad, or ugly. In my story, and I would boldly argue in many at-risk lives seen in the criminal justice system, it is crucial and was crucial for me to build and believe in an ethic that was beyond what racism in America could provide, what my at-risk life provided, and frankly what this cultural identity crisis provided.

Legacy

As funny as it may sound, I didn't know I was an at-risk African American until I went to college and further began my adult life. Let me add that while I knew what racism was and experienced it vividly. I didn't really know how deeply it was rooted and active until I went to college and then later worked in public defender work and saw and researched the greater systematic and historical problems. Further concluding, my racial and cultural maturity didn't really begin until I faced racial adversity or challenge outside of my home of Indianapolis, and I saw that I was really a minority.

Before that time, I thought being raised by a single African mother was the norm. Everyone ate greens and sweet potato pie, everyone had a passion for changing the inner-city of America, and everyone knew Dr. Martin Luther King Jr. was one of America's greatest leaders. Before I left for college, I lived in a city that was 20 percent African American and lived in urban areas of its influence and others. But when I went to the college of my choice, all of a sudden, the world was different, and in my case, I found myself in less of an urban experience earning my education. Now that's the beauty of college, right? It broadens your horizons as you meet different people and think about different ways of thinking. That couldn't be truer in my experience as well, but again, I saw the curse of racism at a different level.

College woke me up to the idea of race at a whole different level and emboldened my sense of legacy and identity. Four scenarios have brought this out among many. One was I began to see literature that was dissing Dr. Martin Luther King Jr. and other African American hallmarks. This blew my mind. Not only that, but I also saw less of a supportive culture for the foundations of what it meant to be African American. You can obviously conclude I did not attend HBCU. I had to begin to better develop a dual-identity and a versatile code-switch game to navigate a culture that I was not used to dominating the majority of everything I did.

Another scenario was going back to "the hood." I must admit it was awkward as I began to grow educationally and within what would become my adult philosophy and way of thinking. The aspects of assimilation or acclimation with old cultural norms and new cultural norms were a fascinating but somewhat difficult journey at times. Certainly, the racial identity development piece was enormous at this time.

Another eye-opening scenario was when I was in a college journalism course. In this course, we were responsible for writing the campus newspaper. I decided to write something about inner city problems and the need for my college to be passionate about and recruit students to make a difference on this behalf. Long story short, if you will, I received a copy of that news in my campus mail, and on was scribbled "nigger rhetoric," and my name was crossed out, and the name "Uncle Tom" along with other scribblings. Now, mind you, this is absolutely nothing compared to what many of my culture went through historically nor compares to the challenge of the champions of the civil rights movement, but for me and at this time, where I had a nostalgic and romantic idea of my college, it was huge. Initially, I did not take this as bad, and my MLK wannabe juices were overflowing with a passion to use this to change the world, if you will. This freshman student was energized and ready to see the transformation on my campus and for the betterment of my college. However, that energy met depression and despondence when the issue was taken to the college president, and you know what's coming next. The administration did very little about the issue. Those who wrote that nonsense and racially sullied my name were caught but were minimally disciplined. They received a "slap on the hand" and resumed their college experience. One person was a top athlete at the institution and had a prominent father who knew the president of the college well. They graduated from this college. I transferred away from that college and lost my post-secondary footing for a while.

This was a minor incident in the grand scheme, but stepping outside of my culture and really enmeshing myself in majority culture pushed me to think deeper and evolve as a person. It highlights a world that still deals with racism and racist tendencies. At that moment and in future moments to come, I had to deal with how I was going to navigate culture and the residuals of racism. It became a journey of study, research, and self-examination to build my ethics and identity on being both of African descent and American birth.

Another anchor in this is that my mother became a central anchor in building my understanding of my cultural context. It was when I got married and became a parent that I really began to appreciate the sacrifice and influence of my mother. My mother, Mary Bailey, embodies all the hallmarks of what has become a strong matriarchal culture in African American life. She is a strict disciplinarian, passionate for her culture, loyal to her family, and has a deep work ethic that, of all things, impacted me. As well, whether it was the *Ebony* and *Jet* magazines on the coffee table, putting me in front of the TV to watch shows like *Roots*, always speaking about African Americans that were breaking the glass ceiling in my childhood and youth, taking me and my brothers to holiday dinners and celebrations with my extended family which featured the breath of food, debate, laughter and the latest discussions of our version of Mahalia Jackson's "How I Got Over," her persistent mentioning of prominent African Americans, or the way she laughed through difficulty and stress, she kept the strained but strong embers of the African American relevance and identity burning bright.

As I began to better learn the plight of African Americans and how they navigated the difficult landscape of racism, I began to appreciate the strength not only of my mother but also of my grandmother and all African American women of her era and situation. The strength that they had to foster and life and limb as women, as African American women, speak to an amazing legacy of strength. It endured as a culture, influence, and ethic that manufactured in me an ethic of perseverance, sacrifice, commitment to culture, and awareness of social issues and their relevance to daily life.

Lastly, there was the influence of my father, grandfathers, uncles, brothers, and friends, the men in my life. These men were distant but while very present. No, this isn't a bashing of them or black men. My father was out of my life at the age of five, and while it may seem that was a trauma, his absence, due to divorce and choice, was so early that I didn't know that was something I was supposed to have or needed in my life. There were attempts at that relationship by my mother early and myself later in life, but it was not as someone endeared to my experience, but as the man who was entitled "my father" and thus deserved welcoming respect without having a connection.

My grandfathers were relics in a museum. One migrated from the south to embrace the jobs of the automobile industry and then became a preacher and the other former military, was always down for grandfatherly influence when over at this house, and he owned what could be described as a "juke-joint" or African American tavern tucked back in the community off of main streets. Both were men of their era, and they were the example of married men in our family.

My uncles, the definition of hustlers—nope, different from what you might think—and those within my culture understand where I'm going. They were former military, had skills to fix any automobile, build a house, were athletes, completed high school, and some of them could even sit you down and speak philosophy with the best of them. But they seemed to be hardened and more impacted by the collateral consequences of racism and chose aberrant lifestyles and lives that helped them best navigate the harsh realities of racism at the time. At any moment, they could hold a great job, fix your car, be model citizens, and then the other struggle with addiction, criminality, anger, and struggle in relationally with their wives, girlfriends, and children, but always, and I mean always, bringing comedy, laughter, and the true definition of cool and swag.

Then there were my closest childhood friends, all African American young men, save one, our Vanilla Ice (Euro-American with swag, and apart from his physical makeup, he could fool you as an African American) at the time. We all, in one way or another, were products of these types of racial, cultural, societal, and family dynamics, and all found our groove, made our way, and enjoyed our way through these various dynamics. For us, it became a place of deep comradery.

Lastly, there are my two older brothers. Frankly, we all were products of our environments, at-risk for sure, racialized indeed, through the challenges of an urban Midwestern city required, and we all built ourselves into our lives and futures differently, all struggled, and while distant from each other, we all are finding our way still in this journey of what I describe as this cultural identity crisis.

Now I went long in describing the men of my life, but as I wrote at the beginning of telling this story of legacy, they were distant while present. History and hype tell the story of the black man in America. By no means does the black man demand undue attention, but when you consider the context of this book and the depth of trauma in the black experience in America, and may I say no less traumatic than that of the black women, but somewhat different, the life of the black man has been complicated as it relates to race, racism and this cultural identity crisis. To the focus of this book and in context with history and a racialized America, the complicated lives of black men are understood. Many of these black men are the men who are overrunning the criminal justice system. I am not suggesting having a culturally competent criminal justice system isn't vastly needed for women in the system, but that said, the criminal justice is extremely failing African American men and will fail continually if it doesn't mandate a culturally responsive process throughout the front and back end of the criminal justice system.

All my life experiences were brought into a greater context, understanding, and enrichment when I began to study my culture, and honestly, many things the public school system failed to teach about the American experience. Most of this occurred late in high school and grew immensely while in college and beyond. It included researching the journey of African Americans from Africa and then understanding the experience of Africans throughout the world. I learned about many individuals, scholars, leaders, philosophies, practices, and the vast and amazing expansion of what it meant to be an African American. Mind you this was not at an HBCU or even in the growing climate, which is growing in demand that we show, teach, and build the history of minorities in our normal American education and daily life. Funny and aging myself, this began almost a decade or more before the age of the internet, and so I had to go old school to study this.

As the personal experiences I mentioned previously, this moment of research, growth, and reflection was pivotal to my identity and purpose. It was a building block to my life that without it, I would be empty of person, purpose, and prosocial output. I would dare say, given the racist history of America and continual challenges, all African Americans, small or great, need this type of experience in their development. I would further argue all of America needs this, at least in our educational traditions. Whether it's handed down from family, through our educational systems, or certainly needed, as I'm explaining in our criminal justice system, this is a necessary anchor to life in America.

All told, as an at-risk child and youth, I didn't have the knowledge and pleasure of reading or being taught the works of Dr. Cross, Dr. Tatum, Dr. DeGruy, and too many to mention to navigate my formative and most crucial years. I didn't have the sociological context of all that has evolved around the former president of Barack Obama to give my journey context. In fact, I had no clue of what I was going through, and for myself here, there, and in various places and through various people, I had to grab my sense of identity and positive legacy of what it meant to be an African American. The outside world wasn't giving it to me, so I grabbed what I could to build what it meant for me to be an African American. Late in high school and then in college, through the backlash of what I was experiencing and seeing, I then had to make a move to better understand the negativity, hype, and frankly, lack of depth I was getting about my culture. As I look back, it was imperative and crucial to develop a cultural ethic and a proper sense of true ethnic-racial identity to navigate my world as an African American man. I was fortunate to be receptive while being truly ignorant, and through my growth bank positivity in my psyche would grow later and push me to my own research and my sense of excellence.

Quite frankly, I was very privileged to skip the usual hardships that were always readily available at my doorstep. Such challenges, and many racialized ones, could have halted my journey of positivity or crippled my ability successfully flourish beyond it. Understanding the true legacy of my people through race, racism, its negative realities and impacts, and its amazing reliance and triumphs is what it means to be an African American, and understanding this is a foundation to requisite abundant living.

Exposure

When in college I had an opportunity to work for the college I attended recruiting students. This opportunity was over the summer when classes were usually out. A team of us traveled to parts of the nation to various areas promoting our college. College began for me an opportunity to see America outside of my Midwestern concrete jungle, and I must express now as an individual who has traveled much since that time, it grew my cultural identity beyond what I can imagine and expanded my identity bandwidth. During this specific opportunity, we visited a camp in Colorado to promote the college. Before that time I had never been to Colorado and I had only seen mountains on the TV or in pictures. Being in the mountains was truly out of reach for my in-person imagination.

The experience I had in those mountains is beyond what I can describe but one moment I can't forget for my at-risk mindset at the time. We drove to the city of Denver and then up into the mountains. As we drove from the Kansas area to reach Denver and our eventual stop, we were on that long stretch on Highway 70. Those who have seen this various times can understand, that as you ascend to the Denver area it's flat and you can't see the mountains for a while but as you get closer the mountains begin to appear. For a kid from a flat city, this was one of the most amazing experiences. I began to see the mountains as we moved closer to Denver, but what flanked that was as the city of Denver came closer, I saw this major American city and it was drowning against the backdrop of the majestic mountains. Personally, it was unbelievable because for me "big city" at least up until that time was more impressive it its awe than this massive piece of nature that was awe-inspiring (take that as deep as you can). As strange as it may sound all of a sudden, I saw life a little differently.

That one experience built many after it and a personal life philosophy that pushed a young man who was comfortable, committed, and frankly loved and admired the "big city" to loving and being committed to nature and natural creation as a source of awe, inspiration, love, and therapy. This writing doesn't permit me to speak to this in its cultural sense and place of minorities being comfortable in natural spaces and its revolution in the African American experience. Truthfully, I couldn't explain it if I tried, but my love for nature blossomed my cultural identity and overall wellness. African American Naturist, Speaker, and Author, Dudley Edmonson gives quality words to what I'm seeking to describe with my lack of ability,

> True freedom lies in wilderness. It's why I've spent much of my life encouraging people of color to explore these spaces.

I was able to experience the mentorship and prowess of Dudley's philosophy as he guided me and other public defenders in a retreat in northern Minnesota. He spoke to this issue of how African Americans and other minorities need to reclaim the natural space as theirs. His book *The Black & Brown Faces in America's Wild Places: African Americans Making Nature and the Environment a Part of Their Everyday Lives*, speaks volumes into this thought and the idea of exposure and claiming a cultural identity that embraces the extraordinary natural places of God's creation. I agree with his perspectives and philosophy as nature of all things has massively expanded my life and impacted me positively. Prior to that one initial experience, I had with my now favorite place to live, Colorado (among other natural places I've been able to frequent and visit), this was culturally unexpectable or better said, unimaginable.

This visual and opportunity piece was significant in my life, and it is significant that at-risk minorities see a life beyond what they experience and an ability to attain that life. There must be a true realization that one of the reasons at-risk minorities continue to commit crime and live negatively is because that's all they know, think themselves to be, or have been defined and categorized to be. Particularly, many people of color see themselves in ways the media portrays them or through the views of a "past" and post-racial America. Changing the script is important through exposing groups to the trueness of their "heritage" and how their "heritage" provides for a healthy identity and healthy living.

In addition to little things like this, practically my faith foundation exposed me to various things that opened my perspective to life beyond myself. As an at-risk youth, I began going to a local northwest side church that had an amazing youth group. I began going there for my own personal hoop ambitions as I was planning to go far in professional basketball like any teenage male in Indiana at the time. Some would beg to differ on this point, but basketball to Indiana was its own religion, and this church had a nice gym and hoops. As I mentioned earlier, an integral aspect of belief systems. This is where it began for me. Part of that was due to this church's dynamic youth activities and events. When I got involved in this youth group, we began to do things I'd never thought of. It was amazingly crazy.

We attended full-week youth camps in the summer outside of my state. We went on college tours of potential colleges around the nation. We had various mind-blowing youth activities at the time that opened my mind to things I'd never seen or thought about. It exposed me to prosocial family dynamics that I did have and various positive father figures and mentors that I didn't have. It exposed me to public speaking and service to mankind. Of all things, it began in me a journey of music basics and music appreciation, and consequently, that has given me pleasure for all genres of music and the various differing cultures that are associated with those genres. It exposed me to foundational life principles I still use today.

Undoubtedly, that was a different day and a different journey than perhaps most. But the exposure was critical for me to look beyond my at-risk identity into things I had no clue I could be or do. It expanded what I thought African Americans were and were to be. It challenged some of the negativity I was growing up with and around and demanded a type of excellence that was not usual to my side of the street. This overzealous faith community, which took in at-risk knuckleheads such as me, could have been a school, a foster parent, a mentorship program, or a neighborhood caring adult, yes, even the criminal justice system. Indeed, it can be the many programs and efforts in criminal justice that can provide not only an anchor of exposure but also academics, legacy, and belief systems for behavior change and, most importantly, a change in historical disparities.

Opportunity

I would be remiss if I did not add another essential anchor in my journey beyond what statistics said I would be, and that is the aspect of opportunity. I would be absolutely wrong to tell the tale of my growth without being given the opportunity to grow out of the circumstances of my life.

Paying absolute and critical homage to those previous people and aspects, America, through various avenues, has provided me the opportunity for education and a career. Not only in day-to-day life, but I was able to go to college on student loans like many, and without that national support, I would not have been able to have the education I now have. I mention this because it seems that in the mid-2000s and beyond, America is more and more in the crossfire of a partisan politics that seems less and less about "we the people" and more "my people." I'm sure some would say, "Wake up, Donavan. It's always been that way." And to that, I would say sure, in the old school sense of self-preservation as I described earlier; however, America, at least on this scale, hasn't seen such a collective effort to be partisan, some saying the very fabric of what it means to be America are being challenge at its foundations. Whether we are a nation that continues to be guided by the "rule of law" is a larger challenge. It could be the continued "by your bootstraps" conservative party agendas that push achievement when, as Dr. King, infamously said on various occasions, it's cruel to tell a bootless person to pick themselves up by the bootstraps.[84] Or the far left or liberal agendas that sometimes lose the ethic of some of America's best foundational hallmarks leaning toward an exclusionary end if one set of people does not embrace another set of people often different from them, often demanding their kind of liberal thought or no other.

America is truly a land of opportunity for all, certainly in its foundational ideal. I was fortunate to live in a time when that ideal did not bar most things from me because of my skin color. As well, I was fortunate enough to begin to build a prosocial and positive identity against the norm at a critical time in my life. Academics, belief systems, legacy, and exposure provided me a foundation to get out of the "the hood," but none of that would mean anything if the "opportunity" to evolve was not present.

My situation could be somewhat unique comparatively to the averages, but many can relate to this unique privilege and opportunity. My personal journey highlights my identity via the previous key factors as a major conglomerate that helped me beyond what statistics predicted for me, and frankly, what my environment set for me. It gave me a vision beyond what was portrayed and experienced and built an internal commitment to strive for true success and impact. However, there are many at-risk minorities just like me who did not have that opportunity and are trapped in the puzzle of the criminal justice system. Historically, they have been trapped, and contemporary unfair practices continue to thrust minorities into the system and, toward the end of this book, keep them there by failing to provide the necessary tools beyond these historical traps. If our country is serious about closing the gap on disparities, if it serious about criminal justice reform, if it is serious about addressing *The New Jim Crow*, indeed if it is serious about America living out its amazing ideals, it must begin to provide per mandated policy a system that better fosters and facilitates opportunity within criminal justice structures to holistically and therapeutically change historical disparities. I ascribe that it must focus on this cultural identity crisis among many things that can be argued about the criminal justice system. The outside change is needed, but it is not enough. It must go deeper in addressing the cultural identity crisis it historically is mostly responsible for creating.

CHAPTER 12

The Ebony Imperative

As mentioned, *Ebony* magazine was a staple in my life growing up. My mother would have it sitting on this old school coffee table that weighed a ton, a table that I worked on launching my first ever steps as a baby. My literal and figurative Armstrong, "That's one small step for a man, one giant leap for mankind..." On this family landmark, not only did she have the current issues of this magazine, but she would have a small stack of the latest issues to accompany the new issues. Not only was this table a cornerstone to launch my physicality, but it was also a center of my cultural launch. As I look back, and like the *Roots* TV series at age five, somehow, this magazine made an early impression on my life. For whatever reason, I would pick it up and look at it and see the world of African American panorama. Funny to me, as I left for college at eighteen years of age and am now older, I go back to my mother's home, sit in her decorated classic living room, complete with African American art, a shrine to the election of Barack Obama, and a mini statue of Mahalia Jackson, I reach over to that same coffee table. Yes, the one I learned to balance, fumble, and stumble and learn to take my first steps by. I reach over and yet still see that *Ebony* magazine.

For those familiar with the magazine, you know it is an Afrocentric magazine. It predates the *BET Channel, the Grio, Essence Magazine,* or the various black mediums of the 2020s; it is a historic and underrated foundation of American culture for sure. It was, in effect, all things black America: entertainment, sports, recent news, and a banner to hold high the pride of being an African American.

As odd as this may sound, there was one issue I looked forward to seeing every year—yes, even as an older adolescent and teenager. It was the 100 Most Influential Black Americans in America Issue, now called the Power 100. This issue was absolutely fascinating to me. Sure, as you can imagine, this issue had people we might imagine to be there on the national American scene. But much more than that, it had doctors, lawyers, teachers, college professions, business leaders, social services leaders, you name it, it had the "successful" black folk that were in American cities throughout the nation. Picture and captions, 100 strong.

Now it might be thought that I picked up this particular issue to be motivated and proud of my Black America. While that was a residual impact and long-term impact, I picked up this issue every year, as if l was looking at the "Alien Magazine" not the *Ebony* magazine. I would gaze at the people with, I'm sure, my mouth gaping open, thinking in a more uneducated urban way, "Who in the heck are these people? I've never seen the likes of such before, wow!" To explain, I didn't see the post-Obama and post-Floyd world when it came to African American positive images and leaders in my at-risk community or even the larger national community. This obviously predated the internet and smartphones.

This is not to say that Indianapolis, a city of rich black history, did not have many, many great African American influential people. It did, and many. But it is to say in my world, I didn't see them much, or I couldn't perceive them through my at-risk lenses. Also, this is not to say I wasn't privileged to the great African American heritage dynamics that are hallmarks in our culture. It is simply to say I was a typical at-risk African American young man who see my world that way.

But other than tremendous matriarchs of my culture, pastors, some ex-military, coaches and the local hustlers of my world, there were not many leaders heralded as influential leaders within my community; or better said, these leaders didn't reach my immediate influence. Nationally, other than historical leaders, such as Dr. Martin

Luther King, as well as other prominent African American leaders of history, there were few contemporary influential people that garnered my attention. Further, I was privy or unfortunately only focused on what many kids get to see more prominently today as influential athletes and entertainers. And for me, that was great, or at least I thought as an aspiring athlete and lover of entertainment, movies, and music: Magic Johnson, Isaiah Thomas, Michael Jackson, LL Cool J, Whitney Houston, Walter Payton, Andre Dawson, Michael Jordan, Bill Cosby, Phylicia Rashad, Debbie Allen, and the list can go on and on and on. But I did not know leaders, ordinary citizens, and professionals that were dental hygienists, lawyers, journalists, news anchors, contractors, teachers, politicians, astronauts, plumbers, business leaders, and that list can go on and on as well. Again, sadly, this is not because there were not any leaders and professionals of that kind—definitely, there were plenty nationally and locally within one of the nation's largest cities in Indianapolis—but within my realm, I didn't see them, or for whatever reason they were not focal point that I grabbed on to practically.

This *Alien Magazine*, and specifically the 100 Most Influential Black Americans or the Power 100 was a journey into an identity I didn't see on the regular. I was awestruck as I saw people who looked like me, who shared my shade of dark pigmentation and wonderful African features. I was in disbelief year after year as I was privileged to see in this magazine that black Americans across the nation were in various and many roles throughout the professional, community, and practical landscapes. These people were real and making a difference. At the time, I couldn't identify with that. It was odd to me. But the brilliance of my mother's direct or indirect placing of that on her old school coffee table was that it would catch the eye and interest of her three boys, and for the youngest of them, it blew my socks off and planted a seed of identity that today I have not forgotten, and that has grown into a tree of reminder and aspiration to be a person of impact and influence. Without that seed of identity, among others, I know for sure I would not be the person I am today, given the at-risk and high-risk circumstances I grew up with.

The battle for identity is intrinsic in minority cultures in America. This can be seen in the very fact that not only at-risk minorities deal with this dynamic, but all descendants of oppressed American cultures also deal with this issue, small or great. This battle is colonized in cultures of America's past racial oppression. "The Seeds of Toby" dynamic while not at the overt and physical level of the days of American slavery, and certainly post POTUS Obama, the game has visibly changed in many ways, one of which had President Biden promise and deliver a black female Supreme Court Justice in his presidency.

Yet, these historic seeds still have profound results as we are centuries away from that original identity "Kunta' knew about from his motherland, Africa. Many black history professionals have written about this identity journey of this proverbial "Kunta vs. Toby" phenomenon. Actor and syndicated columnist Joseph C. Collins expounds on this real historic journey and its personal impact on him in his book. Collins was among many actors and actresses that graced the emphasis *Cosby Show*, which in itself was a huge and historical testament to positive African American identity and thwarted the various stereotypes and notions of negative African American identity. He writes in his book *He Talk Like a White Boy,*

> A number of black authors have written about this duality of consciousness held by black Americans. In his landmark book, The Souls of Black Folk, W. E. B. Dubious wrote, "The Negro ever feel his two-ness-an American, a Negro, two souls, two thoughts, two unreconciled strivings…two warring ideal in one dark body, whose dogged strength alone keeps it from being torn asunder."
>
> A hundred years later, in his book Authentically Black, John McWhorter took this thought another step when he wrote, "A tactic sense reign among a great many black Americans today that the 'authentic' black person stresses

> personal initiative and strength in private, but dutifully takes on the mantle of victimhood as a public face."[85]

Upon these thoughts and authors, Collins gets practically personal. He writes,

> In my forty-plus years, I am certainly familiar with all of the mental gymnastics involved in the attempts at self-definition both DuBois and McWhorter describe. I have equally intimate knowledge of the tightrope walk experienced by so many black people, of being circumspect around white people, ingratiating oneself—making them feel safe?—and being less so around black people. It is not a desire to be perceived black, we simply don't want to be identified as that kind of black...I have heard many white friends say that they have never seen me as black. This is meant as a compliment. I am fairly certain they mean that I like the things they do and laugh at the jokes they make, and I am not given to derailing conversations with a petulant black perspective, during which they must nod and feel my pain. My response to these compliments is that while I am appreciative of their acceptance, I am black. So, here is yet another pose in the mental yoga that black people practice; Striving to realize our individual humanity while still holding tight to some portion of our racial identity. (I am quite certain my white friends and neighbors do not put themselves through these mental acrobatics. However, every black person I know is constantly involved in this type of intricate analysis.

This identity is a key piece of the lives of the American minority. Of the many current authorities on the African American journey, there is probably none more profound, authentic, and "hip" than the work of Dr. Michael Eric Dyson. He has authored various books, commentates on various news shows, and is currently a professor of sociology at Vanderbilt University. In his book *Debating Race: with Michael Eric Dyson*, he mentions a key understanding that solidifies the theory of this report. Speaking on the defining issue with regard to race and ethnicity, he mentions,

> People are often posing question to people of color and women, "Are you Latino first or are you American? Are you black first or are you an American? Are you women first or are you an American?" And the reality is the simultaneity of our identities; they converge together, they come to us at the same time. And many people have not been trained to think about or to understand the complexity of that convergence. And yet, we must pay attention to the particular ways in which our identities are shaped as a result of race and ethnicity. So, the tension between what we have been and where we have come from, and what we are now, continues to express itself, I think, with lethal intensity, with a ferocity that is indexed in the following: that people simply keep asking the question, "Haven't we been there done that, and can't we move forward?" But until we wrestle with those demons that have shaped and framed us, we will scarcely be able to embrace the full measure of our humanity as citizens in American society.[86]

If this type of dynamic is buried in the identity minority cultures such as the African American, a dynamic with many layers described in the culture as a whole, my culture, how much more is this a vital issue with those at-risk minorities that overflow in America's criminal justice system? Couple that with the fact that the criminal justice system has been used to perpetuate racist practices against at-risk minorities for centuries. This speaks to a quandary that is deep, and if the criminal justice system and other entities that deal with those from or involved with the criminal justice system desire to rehabilitate, treat, and change the statistics and cycle of criminality and incarceration, a focus on the ethnocentric identity is paramount, a focus that leads to policies and practices.

Throughout this book, I have interwoven some aspects of my personal journey because I am or was that at-risk African American young man who somehow made it out of my at-risk conditions into what is described as the American dream. While many dynamics can be entered and debated as to what it is that gives a person the ability to make it out of negative environments, whether it be the at-risk Native American, the at-risk Hispanic descendant of immigrants, or the at-risk refugee from Sudan or Somalia, discovering one's true identity was imperative and powerful to support and motivate a prosocial life amid inward and outward racial constraints to muffle that identity. I mentioned *academics*, *belief systems*, *legacy*, *exposure*, and *opportunity* as essential elements for my identity and consequent actions. I further espouse these aspects as essential elements to an inferior criminal justice insufficient in its attempts to rehabilitate at-risk minorities that engulf the criminal justice system. Personally, this described cultural identity crisis was real to me, and fostering a positive identity development while dealing with aspects described as "soul wounds" or historical trauma was vital for my life.

Professionally, I work daily with clientele with these issues. Having worked in public defender offices in Minnesota, Arizona, and Colorado and further in various professions in the criminal justice system, it is clear that racist tendencies have affected the criminal justice system through its deep history of incarcerating disproportionate amounts of minorities. And evidently, this issue has taken such a long, historic, and now entrenched and multi-layered impact on at-risk minorities that it has impacted their identity to a place where the criminal justice system is an ingrained piece of their, perhaps better said our cultural normality. This is plainly sick.

I'm a practitioner, advocate, and social worker within America and, more specifically, public defender work, and while experienced in this field with a doctorate in education, I'm not a psychologist, psychiatrist, sociologist, politician, probation officer, judge, lawyer or even a guru of my own African American culture, but as the age-old saying goes, "It does not take a rocket scientist." Merely, I hope I have been able to advocate for the fact that "it does not take a rocket scientist" to understand that racist tendencies and their historic enculturation and grasp on clientele within the criminal justice system have had a massive toll on minority populations. This has impacted poverty, employment, mental health, education, economic health, and family systems of cultures of people. More importantly, from my standpoint, this has impacted the identity of most at-risk minorities living with generations and generations impacted by racism and the criminal justice system.

Conclusively, while the criminal justice system has been historically racist and still grapples with racist tendencies, and while there are other issues that affect this problem, such as the culture of poverty and the need to address mental health, there is a larger issue after decades of systematic racial issue and disproportionate incarceration and probation of minorities, that issue is that many at-risk minorities identify with criminality as a part of their normality or have been forced to live in the box of this identity. With respect to obvious issues all at-risk populations face and the traditional treatment components necessary for optimum corrections and treatment, when it comes to the historic, disproportionate, and embedded culture of minorities in the criminal justice system, addressing one's identity from a cultural standpoint is a core issue that is overlooked in most traditional in-patient and outpatient correctional and treatment programming. There is a cultural identity crisis with at-risk minorities and a failure to address this aspect adequately within correctional and treatment structures. This cultural identity crisis is an important barrier in the criminal justice system as it relates to treatment, rehabilitation, and corrective processes to assist with changing this weathered and deep-rooted culture of minorities in the criminal justice system.

Moreover, it is an issue related to recidivism, public safety, and the many aspects that have been unearthed again through the Black Lives Matter movement, unrest in urban cities, the cry for change, and the quest for criminal justice reform. It is at the bedrock of the "what's next" in correlation to many researched and debated ideas on this issue. It is time that all fifty states and the federal criminal justice system not only recognize and politically support the current hallmarks of criminal justice reform, which is more of a front-end approach. But also, a corrective and therapeutic ideal, which is a holistic back-end approach seeking to stifle the ravaging collective collateral consequences on cultures of at-risk minorities from oppressed cultures. This will take the criminal justice system literally placing on the "coffee tables" in every prison and jail, if you will, the *Ebony* magazines of our day: direct, indirect, symbolic, therapeutic, and embedded in correctional, court, and probation programming.

CHAPTER 13

Seeing Is Achieving

As a maturing American, there are two distinct "do you remember where you were when" moments that overshadow all the moments that I recovered from my aged memory. One is now the past tragedy of the 911 attacks in 2001, and the other is the night President Barack Obama won the presidency of the United States and, more specifically, the day of his consequent inauguration as the forty-fourth president of the United States.

I remember well, going over to my mother's house around lunch on my workday, Inauguration Day. On that day, not only was my mother there, a woman typical of her generation holding the banner of African American heritage for her three boys as a single mother, but also my Uncle Edward was there, a hardened black power, Vietnam veteran, and of African American descent. He is a brilliant man, however hampered by the urban unrest, racism, his many bouts with the criminal justice system, and the cultural identity crisis of his era. Both faced overt racism in ways I couldn't understand.

Descriptive of my family and my uncle's and mother's, they are never usually short on words when together. These folks often debated and argued deep into the night about crazy issues, waking me up numerous times in my adolescence and youth. This was especially true when politics were the topic of discussion. But oddly, when the broadcast came on, shown on every major network, for my mother, CNN was the channel. President Barack Obama was being sworn in. There was a silence in that living room that I rarely, if ever, heard when my uncle and mother were together. They watched in awe as the man of color, flanked by his beautiful African American wife and two beautiful daughters, was sworn in. I watched in awe as well but with a keen eye for these two people and their awestruck nature. It was amazing to watch people who had seen some of the ugliest things in their history as it relates to racism, and now they had a true moment of silence and speechlessness as the glass ceiling on identity was broken having a president of African descent being sworn in to lead the United States.

As the age of President Barack Obama has ended and many will continue to splice, slice, dice, and recreate his role in American history. As history unfolds, this will be written more eloquently in the passage of time and the many that orate and write about his existence. But as my kids and I had the privilege of seeing Mount Rushmore in 2016 and gazing on the identity of four men who impacted this country and etched in a mountainside, it is not their politics we remember but the critical place in our history and the identity they hold for us as Americans. President Barack Obama held for us the epiphany of the American ideal with eloquence and brilliance at the highest office on earth. He embodied physically both Euro-American and African American. The presence of him, his wife. and children held for us an identity with which many will aspire for ages to come. Since this glass has now been broken, many who thought ascending to such height was impossible will put their political hat in the ring to be all that they can be. To a lesser degree, but just as impactful, once America takes time to embrace it, Vice President Kamala Harris has and will have the same impact.

Moreover, while President Obama enjoyed some privilege, he, too, was an at-risk young man of color with an absent father for key parts of his life. This is a theme we see all too much are familiar with in the US criminal justice system and keenly among the disparity totals plaguing the system. Yet he now stands as a model that overcame his at-risk upbringing, bicultural identity, and the various stigmas of being an African American to ascend to the presidency and historical influence.

The story of Alex Haley's "Kunta Kinte" in his *Roots* saga is now and has been for centuries the story of America. It represents various similar stories of the African journey to the Americas. What is seen in this historic saga was not only the beginning of the journey of holding on to African "roots" but how, in a magnificent way, Africans adapted, assimilated, and metamorphosed from being Africans to African Americans. POTUS Obama is the symbolic representation of this.

Despite the end of his presidency and aside from the politics associated with his tenure, President Obama stands as the most symbolic representation of the dream and hope of slaves. More broadly, he symbolically represents the ultimate coverage of the oppressed and the oppressor, being of Euro-American descent and African descent. In the context of what has gone on in this country recently, and for centuries, this is tremendous for the American concept.

This is the age of Maya Angelou's "the dream and hope of the slave." Even among serious challenges, some of which bring a fear of a retracting America on race, this is the day of a dream of America fuller. But to reach the essence of what POTUS Obama represents for all of America, it cannot be full of such disparities as described. This is the time to make sure each African American and at-risk minority knows that their value is far beyond the normalization of race, crime, poverty, and dysfunction. This is the time for them to know that that they, too, can aspire beyond what they've seen, been forced to see, have acquiesced to or have been forced to given in to.

As the system will find the latest and greatest evidence-based practices, assessment and therapy to measure disproportionality, as the public and private discussion raises within criminal justice structures, as the conversation ensues about race, the role of police, urban city challenges, criminal justice. As discussion after discussion is had, the plight of the precious lives of African Americans that are lost so tragically almost as the extension of the horrors of past American slavery. Yes, as the system looks for answers, finds answers, and doubles over on the same rhetoric for decades, it has not found an answer to stop the plague of disparities in the criminal justice system. It cannot skip the need for a more engrained and holistic approach toward disparities and criminal justice reform.

As this book has espoused among the various valiant and research-based attempts to change the plight of race and disparities in criminal justice, it cannot be absent infusing and inundating the criminal justice system with the identity of the Obama generation. At-risk minorities need to know their history, their value, and their potential. They need to know the truth about what racism is and what racism is not. Further, they need to develop the tools to not only advocate for equality, a front end, and reactive approach, but they also need to cultivate knowledge on how to acclimate, assimilate, and thrive in a country that has marginalized them and is struggling to dissociate holistically from that history. This then must be coupled with access to opportunity, education, and exposure to the vastness of what it means to be an African American and what it means to be an American.

For those within the criminal justice system, there is no question there is a need for behavior modification effort, therapy, treatment, mental health assessment and invention, and yes, corrective action and punishment. But aside from these measures, the system must adopt among its philosophy and hiring practices a full onslaught of efforts to give at-risk minorities a sense of their true identity. If the system is bold enough to admit or evolve to the place where it owns the aspects of a historic racist criminal justice system, as the documentary *13th* and the efforts of Michelle Alexander have exposed. It then must also adopt efforts to change this plight of how African Americans and other at-risk minorities go into the system. This means a creative look at the aspects of identity and its influence in changing the deplorable American incarceration situation.

Truly, African Americans and other minorities trapped in the criminal justice system "cannot aspire to be what they cannot see," as Drs. Sampson Davis, Rameck Hunt, and George Jenkins showed us with their infamous books, documentaries, and community outreach.[87] Politics aside, President Obama and the American vote gave this country a glimpse of a new day. A new day that grew to Vice President Kamala Harris and America's first African American female

Supreme Court Justice, Judge Ketanji Brown Jackson. As politics fade and history takes an honest look at what Obama meant in the context of the American ideal, it will have seen and embraced the essence that this man embodied as he was the convergence of the oppressed and the oppressor unified at the most powerful position in the world.

Every youth and adult in the criminal justice system must be taught to know and have access to attain the identity of an Obama America. To date, the presidency of Barack Obama is the most powerful symbol of a past and present America and the epitome of the "we the people" standard of our Constitution.

CHAPTER 14

Ode to Uncle Ed's

One day, about fifteen years ago, I was passing through the hallway of my public defender office, and one of our lead and best attorneys crossed my path and said to me, "Hey, Donny, I met your uncle today in jail. He is really a nice guy Yes, you are allowed to laugh here. Anyways, this was my Uncle Ed mentioned in the previous chapter. Now coming from this attorney, every bit of that was meant in the best of ways and nothing negative. He is a tremendous person and was a true attorney for the needy. However, for myself, I had to inwardly smile, laugh, and minimally cringe as my Uncle Ed was now a part of my then Third District Southeast Minnesota Public Defender clientele. Not in any way being a native of Minnesota but from Indianapolis, this made this all the more hilarious and professionally awkward.

Now the "awkward" is probably understood, but the "hilarious," I realize likely not so much. To explain, Uncle Ed was one of those "uncles," right (many know what I'm alluding to here…) that lived life with such intensity and verbosity, and that coupled with an intense aura of the context that this book has sought to bring about. Moreover, he had his own tremendous frailties ta-boot, with this opposite brilliance, life perspective, and the passion of a 1960's civil rights activist. He had a street PhD by his own self-study and honestly could spar with those of legitimate terminal degrees on issues of philosophy, religion, politics, and psychology. To debate with him was to admit defeat before a debate began. Then, he could go outside and repair your car and repair mostly anything that needed repair. He had a swag of his day, which they called "cool," and respectfully said to our modern times, where we better respect women and learning to better respect women. Let's just say he never had a problem getting a date. He was a military man and hardened by Vietnam and the challenges of being a black man in the military at that time. No, he didn't speak about that military experience. I heard the tales of its amazing challenge from my mother and never from him.

He was a symbol of sorts for many black men of his generation. They invoked the yin and yang of the African American man who grew up in America's turbulent 1960s and then had to find a way forward in the advanced continued racism of his era. And somehow, this was all done in the context of extreme swag, true adaptability, and "the hustle." He was the "dark comedy" on full display that was challenging but cherished.

In the early part of 2017, Uncle Ed passed away. As death can do, it sparked a remembrance and reflection of the dearly departed. In an interesting way, it can push a person to categorize the impact and the overall influence of a lost loved one or close friend. Strangely, his passing seemed to hold much significance because Uncle Ed was this all-consuming, controversial, and full-of—life individual that had his share of enemies within and without my family. While he was belabored with much of what my clients often struggle with, drugs, alcohol, dysfunctional relationships, and undiagnosed mental health issues, this troubled Vietnam Veteran was the embodiment of many of the African American man or the at-risk African American man.

Of many things, he was what I would call a reactionary racist, meaning he was not fond of the Euro-American culture due to the history of racism and the racism he experienced in his lifetime. This was always hilarious to me because he had this reactionary demeanor toward Euro-Americans while skillfully navigating and befriending those of the United States dominant heritage; and may I add, while notoriously having various committed girlfriends of Euro-American heritage in his lifetime, this always puzzled me. How could he hate white people, or Euro-Americans, but date their women?

Nonetheless, at his passing and in not-so-positive forms, succumbing to chemical dependency and life lived so roughly, this man from my at-risk upbringing was a centerpiece of what a man was in my familial upbringing. Today, Uncle Ed would likely be diagnosed with anxiety, depression, PTSD, and Bipolar. This old-school "papa was a rolling stone" overcame the harsh realities of his time and somehow kept a deep and brilliant mind. That, too, was a puzzling thing, as his demons seemed to overshadow his potential and inborn prowess. But also, and much more impactful, it seems the challenges of race and the criminal justice system of his time were too high an obstacle to overcome to maximize his potential. From the military to civilian life, he had to struggle with the criminal justice system as well as many black men of his time, and as we are speaking today, many black men now disproportionately in jails, prisons, probation caseloads, and in our courts.

While he offended many, was a hellion of sorts in many respects, and paved a path of his own destruction all across his many transient travels across the United States, and while many might conclude that this type of life is not the best example to be mentioning as a positive role model, he was as much of an object of his own choosing as much as a sad statistic of racial realities of the criminal justice system. And while he was a "one in three" black man caught up in the criminal justice system and its lengthy and deep collateral consequences that were much more overt in his day. He was the image of manhood in our family and many similar families. While captivated by his own failures, he was too captivated by racism, the criminal justice system, and the scourge it could take on one's life. He led a tough life, but we understood him, his journey, and his mark on our family life and culture.

As I've sought to do this book, while this has been as much about calling for and showing a distinct example of holistic criminal justice reform, it is also a telling my story of how I missed what many at-risk African Americans go through and how it can provide one answer to stop this dreaded disparity issues of the United States criminal justice system. The "Uncle Eds" are plenty—yes, different from generation to generation—and surely, in the 2020s and beyond, morphed in different ways. Yes, young and old, most imprisoned by personal choices, then some inappropriately through systematic anchors. Many are challenges but also via the culprits of racism and how the criminal justice system can hang like a hundred-pound weight on the shoulders of a young black man seeking to move forward in the journey toward personal success.

Those familiar with the story of "Uncle Ed" can surmise that his life died tragically, essentially besieged by and overran by the life he lived. A brilliant life extinguished too soon and without full fruit. A life in the criminal justice system and race intertwined owned a major piece of his life. His story is repeated over and over in everyday life.

The truth is the life my Uncle Ed lived, and many at-risk African Americans and at-risk minorities live, statistically was supposed to be my life. I, too, was to be that "one in three" African American young man in the constraints and obstacles of race and the criminal justice system, and that was how I was to navigate my life. But despite the challenges and the reality of the "1 in 3" African American males being succumbed by the criminal justice system, there was a deeper identity that called from the time of the actual "roots" and spoke in me a much greater existence that I experienced and what statistics would predict for me. That identity pushed me beyond the cultural identity crisis to a life I never thought imaginable. This is my journey to "make it out", if you will, and while different than others, it stands in my professional opinion as a key discourse (as espoused in this book) to change Michelle Alexander's *The New Jim Crow*, the issues brought out in the *13th* documentary, deeper issues of Black Lives Matter, the achievement gap in American schools, the call for change, criminal justice reform and that vast issues of urban unrest in inner cities.

All these movements and issues to address, while needing to change the systems of racism, must understand that, in many ways, these historic systematic problems have done damage and still hold many minority lives under lock and key. And to this book's premise, under the psychological lock and key of this cultural identity crisis. America experienced one of its great days on January 1, 1863. The fight for equality was won, and African American slaves were freed. However, as Juneteenth shows us slaves in Galveston, Texas, did not know this until 1865. Moreover, the greater issue of equity began, and while by law, equality was afforded, many slaves had to almost live as slaves to survive after 1863, not to mention the rigged laws that began via the criminal justice system to keep blacks enslaved through crazy laws that railroaded African Americans to jails and prison and thus still servants of the state.

The battle for Black Lives Matter, the call for change, and the current criminal justice reform efforts cannot end with wins on the front end of that battle to change the system alone. Those are great wins and mini, if you will, 1863s. There is a greater work to also do because of the collateral consequences of historic systematic racism by the criminal justice system, and addressing this cultural identity crisis is key to that.

As mentioned previously, the late Dr. Maya Angelo penned, in my opinion, the best motivational essence of this identity in her well-known Poem, *Still I Rise*, and it holds within its beautiful rhythmic words this,

> Bringing the gifts that my ancestors gave, I
> am the dream and the hope of the slave.[88]

In this one sentence is the voice of a positive identity that understands the journey, the struggle, racism, the legacy of strong identity, and sacrifice for a better future for African Americans. While Kunta Kinte sought to keep his name, to hold on to what he and his culture were, it now, via the struggle, speaks forward to every African American to remember the depth and wealth of being African and now African American. It speaks to the Uncle Eds of this life to understand they are much more than their past, racism, and even what the criminal justice system can heap upon an individual and a culture. It's a story, as presented previously, that each African American man and woman needs to hear in every jail and prison. Further, it speaks to a greater principle of identity or cultural identity that everyone needs to know in jails and prisons in hopes of realizing that their identity is tied to something much higher than their past actions, challenging future stereotypes, and the latest evidence-based practices predict. If this notion of a cultural identity crisis or thought of bolstering positive ethnic-racial identity permeates jails, prisons, courts, corrections philosophy, and probation caseloads, it would significantly provide an amazing platform that would drastically change disparities and its hideous collateral consequences. It would give an encouraging path to the Uncle Eds, if you will, to not settle, hustle through, and even glamorize the celebrated swag of criminality and badboyism of what the challenges of racism mixed with the criminal justice system often produces. It is the seventeenth century, René Descartes, "I think therefore I am" imperative anchor that must permeate all efforts at criminal justice reform.

The story of Alex Haley's "Kunta Kinte" in his *Roots* saga is now and has been for centuries the story of America. In various contexts, the story of the Africans now in America has taken on a beautiful panorama in American history. This includes other disparities we see with Latino Americans and Native Americans. The issues of this book are not African American, Native American, or Hispanic American. While cultural in its disproportionate make-up, it is American in its construction and responsibility. Until the issues of this cultural identity crisis and its various thoughts and implications within the criminal justice system become American, adopted as our problem, and powerfully supported by state and federal policies, disparities will continue. Criminal justice reform is American and must be reformed holistically via federal and state policy committed to cultural competence or the "dream and hope," or America will continue to be broken. No American culture can truly flourish when it occupies 36 percent to 40 percent of jails and prisons while it only occupies 13 percent of the population.

For African Americans, we are all still on a journey of navigating the seeds of Toby and bettering our place internally and externally in America and the world. Scholars, theologians, psychologists, therapists, sociologists, educators, and social workers well above my pay grade have expounded on issues of the ethnic-racial identity and its individual and collective impact on many Americans. With respect to this humble and meager attempt at addressing the cultural identity crisis, their works, some espoused here, must inundate the criminal justice system for the needed change many are attempting and calling for. As said, there must be an "I think, therefore I am" anchor of the criminal justice system to address the continual issues overly apparent. The thoughts of this book are therefore written as a holistic "call to action" and submitted as chief anchors to brainstorm and formulate real changes in the American criminal justice system and in America as a whole.

In the previously mentioned criminal justice program I used to test and live-out the concepts of this book was the use of Hip Hop songs and genre; as noted a huge medium for this type of thought and therefore a stellar prop for the curriculum. One song we used to highlight our group conversations was, *G.O.D. (Gaining One's Definition),* by legendary rap artist, Common, and exceptional vocalist, CeeLo Green. Their musical talent and depth made this a powerful addition to our attempts to unpack this notion of *The Seeds of Toby,* in efforts to assist our clients with better lives. Its words are optimum and apropos for marginalized cultures that override the criminal justice system and as they fight both inward and outward challenges to ascend to Dr. King's "Somebodiness". Equally so and toward the purpose of this dialogue, they speak forward to the deeper focus that the modern-day criminal justice system must facilitate and unpack in their efforts, or lack thereof, to offset and assist with forever changing the historical cultural disparities in American jails, prisons and probation caseloads. These infamous and masterful artists speak volumes about this song without even hearing it, but its full depth, sound, style and rhythm puts it at a whole new level. As the saying goes, mere words cannot do it justice, but with a segment of this song we conclude and commence,

"Let me voice my concern
So many of my fellow brothers have given themselves
a title that their actions didn't earn
Our ignorance is in the same breath as our innocence
Subconsciously, seeking to find an impressionable mind to convince

I've finally come to the realization why Black
people are in the worse place
'Cuz it's hard to correct yourself when you don't
know who you are in the first place…"

NOTES

Introduction

1 Brown, M., "Trump Says His Criminal Indictments Boosted His Appeal to Black Voters," Retrieved from *Associated Press*, February 24, 2024, https://apnews.com/article/trump-black-conservative-south-carolina-primary-aa1155c31bfc3b397a32b33eff04ada8

2 Alexander, M., *The New Jim Crow: Mass Incarceration in the Age of Colorblindness* (New York, NY: The New Press, 2010).

3 Hinton, E., Hendersen, L., and Reed, C., "An Unjust Burden: The Disparate Treatment of Black Americans in the Criminal Justice System," Vera Institute of Justice (2018). Retrieved from https://www.vera.org/downloads/publications/for-the-record-unjust-burden-racial-disparities.pdf.

Chapter 1

4 Hartney, C., "US Rates of Incarceration: A Global Perspective," *National Council on Crime and Delinquency* (2006).

5 NAACP, "Misplaced Priorities: Over Incarcerate, Under Educate" (2011).

6 The Sentencing Project, "Report of the Sentencing Project to the United Nations Human Rights Committee: Regarding Racial Disparities in the United States Criminal Justice System" (2013).

7 Kerby, S., "The Top 10 Most Startling Facts About People of Color and Criminal Justice in the United States," The Center for American Progress (2012).

8 Nellis, A., "The Color of Justice 2016 Report, the Sentencing Project" (2016).

9 Motivans, M., "Federal Justice Statistics, 2019," Bureau of Justice Statistics (2019).

10 Gramlich, J., "The Gap between the Number of Blacks and Whites in Prison Is Shrinking," retrieved from The Pew Research Center (April 30, 2019), https://

www.pewresearch.org/short-reads/2019/04/30/shrinking-gap-between-number-of-blacks-and-whites-in-prison/#:~:text=In%202017%2C%20there%20were%201%2C549,have%20declined%20substantially%20since%202007.

11 Wagner, P., and Walsh, A., "States of Incarceration: The Global Context 2016," The Prison Policy Initiative (2016).

12 Bureau of Justice Statistics, "Prisoners in 2022—Statistical Tables" (November 2023), https://bjs.ojp.gov/document/p22st.pdf

13 Ghandnoosh, N., "One in Five: How Mass Incarceration Deepens Inequality and Harms Public Safety," retrieved from The Sentencing Project (January 16, 2024), https://www.sentencingproject.org/publications/one-in-five-how-mass-incarceration-deepens-inequality-and-harms-public-safety/.

14 Wertheimer, J., "Racial Disparities Persist in Many US Jails," retrieved from The Pew Charitable Trust (May 16, 2023), https://www.pewtrusts.org/en/research-and-analysis/issue-briefs/2023/05/racial-disparities-persist-in-many-us-jails.

15 Sawyer, W., and Wagner, P., Mass Incarceration: The Whole Pie 2024, retrieved from Prison Policy Initiative (March 14, 2024), https://www.prisonpolicy.org/reports/pie2024.html#:~:text=It%27s%20no%20surprise%20that%20people,14%25%20of%20all%20U.S%20residents.

16 The White House of Barack Obama, "Criminal Justice Reform" (2021), retrieved from https://obamawhitehouse.archives.gov/issues/criminal-justice-reform.
Somanader, T., "President Obama: "Why We Must Rethink Solitary Confinement," The White House of Barack Obama (2016).

17 Federal Bureau of Prisons, "An Overview of the First Step Act" (2018), retrieved from https://www.bop.gov/inmates/fsa/overview.jsp.

18 The White House of Joseph Biden, "FACT SHEET: The Biden-Harris Administration's Work to Make Our Communities Safer and Advance Effective, Accountable Policing" (February 7, 2023), retrieved from https://www.whitehouse.gov/briefing-room/statements-releases/2023/02/07/fact-sheet-the-biden-harris-administrations-work-to-make-our-communities-safer-and-advance-effective-accountable-policing/.

Chapter 2

19 Tracy Huling, "Building a Prison Economy in Rural America," retrieved from Prison Policy Initiative, 2002, https://www.prisonpolicy.org/scans/building.html.

20 Berson, S. B., "Beyond the Sentence—Understanding Collateral Consequences," *National Institute of Justice Journal* (2013): 25–28.

21 Western, B., and Pettit, B., "Collateral Costs: Incarceration's Effect on Economic," The Pew Charitable Trusts, 2010.

22 Arditti, J., "Parental Incarceration and the Family: Psychological and Social Effects of Imprisonment on Children, Parents, and Caregivers," New York University Press, 2014.

[23] Martin, E., "Hidden Consequences: The Impact of Incarceration on Dependent Children," *National Institue of Justice Journal* (2017): 1–7, retrieved from https://www.ojp.gov/pdffiles1/nij/250349.pdf.

Chapter 3

[24] Meet the Press. "Giuliani and Dyson Argue Over Violence in Black Communities," retrieved from NBC News, November 23, 2014, https://www.nbcnews.com/video/giuliani---dyson-argue-over-violence-in-black-communities-362441283717.

[25] *The Chris Rock Show*, "How Not to Get Your Ass Kicked by the Police," retrieved from YouTube, July 14, 2024, https://www.youtube.com/watch?v=uj0mtxXEGE8

[26] Martin Luther King Jr., "Martin Luther King, Jr., "What Is Your Life's Blueprint?" retrieved from YouTube, October 26, 1967, https://www.youtube.com/watch?v=ZmtOGXreTOU
Martin Luther King Jr. "What Is Your Life's Blueprint?" Retrieved from *The Seattle Times*, July 14, 2024, https://projects.seattletimes.com/mlk/words-blueprint.html.

Chapter 4

[27] Saleebey, D. "The Strengths Perspective: Putting Possibility and Hope to Work in Our Practice," in B. W. White, K. M. Sowers, and C. N. Dulmus, *The Comprehensive Handbook of Social Work and Social Welfare* (pp. 123–142) (Hoboken, New Jersey: John Wiley & Sons, Inc), 2008, retrieved from https://www.hzu.edu.in/uploads/2020/9/Comprehensive%20Handbook%20of%20Social%20Work%20and%20Social%20Welfare.pdf.

[28] Krestan, J. A. E., *Bridges to Recovery: Addiction, Family Therapy, and Multicultural Treatment* (New York, NY: The Free Press, 2000).

[29] Shearer, R. A., and King, P. A., "Multicultural Competencies in Probation—Issues and *Federal Probation*," 2004, retrieved from https://www.uscourts.gov/sites/default/files/fed_probation_june_2004.pdf

[30] Eisen, L. B., "The 1994 Crime Bill and Beyond: How Federal Funding Shapes the Criminal Justice System," retrieved from The Brennan Center for Justice (September 9, 2019), https://www.brennancenter.org/our-work/analysis-opinion/1994-crime-bill-and-beyond-how-federal-funding-shapes-criminal-justice.

Chapter 5

[31] Saint-Exupéry, A. D., "Flight to Arras. II," *The Atlantic* (February 1942), retrieved from https://www.theatlantic.com/magazine/archive/1942/02/flight-to-arras-ii/653775/.

32 *Merriam-Webster*, "Identity," July 3, 2024, retrieved from https://www.merriam-webster.com/dictionary/identity.

33 *Merriam-Webster*, "Crisis," July 3, 2024, retrieved from https://www.merriam-webster.com/dictionary/crisis.

34 *Merriam-Webster*, "Cultural," July 3, 2024, retrieved from https://www.merriam-webster.com/dictionary/cultural.

35 *Merriam-Webster*, "Culture," July 3, 2024, retrieved from https://www.merriam-webster.com/dictionary/culture.

36 Cherry, K., "Biography of Erik Erikson [1902–1994], February 23, 2023, retrieved from Verywell Mind: https://www.verywellmind.com/erik-erikson-biography-1902-1994-2795538.

37 Tiwari, K. L., "Identity Crisis—Indian English Fiction of Post 1980s," *International Journal of English and Literature* (2013): 6–10.

38 Erickson, E., "Autobiographic Notes on the Identity Crisis," *Daedalus*, (1970): 730–759, retrieved from https://www.jstor.org/stable/pdf/20023973.pdf.

39 Cherry, K., "How to Recognize and Cope With an Identity Crisis," April 11, 2023, retrieved from Verywell Mind: https://www.verywellmind.com/what-is-an-identity-crisis-2795948.

40 Holloway, K. F., *Codes of Conduct: Race, Ethics, and the Color of Our Character* (New Brunswick, New Jersey: Rutgers University Press, 1996).

Chapter 6

41 Bailey, T., "Issues in American Indian Health," July 19, 2024, retrieved from University of Minnesota Duluth: https://www.d.umn.edu/cla/faculty/tbacig/studproj/is3099/nahealth/paper.html.

42 Lambert, C., "Trails of Tears, and Hope," *Havard Magazine*, March 2008, retrieved from https://www.harvardmagazine.com/2008/03/trails-of-tears-and-hope-html.

43 Sotero, M., "A Conceptual Model of Historical Trauma: Implications for Public Health Practice and Research," *Journal of Health Disparities Research and Practice* (2006): 93–108.

44 Kirmayer, L. J., Joseph P. Gone, and Moses, J., "Rethinking Historical Trauma," *Transcultural Psychiatry* (2014), doi:https://doi.org/10.1177/1363461514536358.

45 Alexander, J. C., Eyerman, R., Giesen, B., Smelser, N. J., and Sztompka, P., *Cultural Trauma and Collective Identity* (Oakland, CA: University of California Press, 2004).

46 DeGruy, J., *Post Traumatic Slave Syndrome, Revised Edition: America's Legacy of Enduring Injury and Healing* (Joy Degruy Publications Inc., 2017).

47 Tatum, B. D., *Why Are All the Black Kids Sitting Together in the Cafeteria?: And Other Conversations About Race* (Basic Books, 2017).

48 Peacock, T., *To Be Free: Understanding and Eliminating Racism* (Afton, MN: Afton Historical Society Press, 2010).

[49] Tatum, B. D., *Why Are All the Black Kids Sitting Together in the Cafeteria?: And Other Conversations About Race* (Basic Books, 2017).

[50] Yip, T., "Ethnic/Racial Identity-A Double-Edged Sword? Associations With Discrimination and Psychological Outcomes," *Current Directions in Psychological Science* (2018): 170–175.

[51] Rivas-Drake, D., Markstrom, C., Syed, M., Lee, R. M., Umaña-Taylor, A. J., Yip, T., … French, S., "Ethnic and Racial Identity in Adolescence: Implications for Psychosocial, Academic, and Health Outcomes," *Child Development* (2014): 40–57.

[52] Santos, C. E., Kornienko, O., and Rivas-Drake, D., "Peer Influence on Ethnic-Racial Identity Development: A Multi-Site Investigation," *Child Development* (2017): 725–742.

[53] Wantchekon, K. A., Umaña-Taylor, Sladek, A. J., Michael R. McDermott, E. R., and Updegraff, K. A., "Adolescents' Ethnic-Racial Centrality Moderates Effect of School-Based Intervention on Ethnic-Racial Identity Exploration," *Developmental Psychology* (2021): 432–442.

Chapter 7

[54] Eisen, L. B., "Report Reveals Ineffectiveness of Mass Incarceration," retrieved from Brennan Center for Justice, February 23, 2015, https://www.brennancenter.org/our-work/analysis-opinion/report-reveals-ineffectiveness-mass-incarceration.

[55] National Institute of Justice, "Recidivism," July 19, 2024, retrieved from https://nij.ojp.gov/topics/corrections/recidivism#:~:text=Recidivism%20is%20one%20of%20the,intervention%20for%20a%20previous%20crime.

[56] Benecchi, L., "Recidivism Imprisons American Progress," retrieved from Harvard Political Review, August 8, 2021, https://harvardpolitics.com/recidivism-american-progress/.

[57] Benecchi, L., "Recidivism Imprisons American Progress," retrieved from Harvard Political Review, August 8, 2021, https://harvardpolitics.com/recidivism-american-progress/.

[58] King, W. R., Holmes, S. T., Henderson, M. L., and Latessa, E. J., "The Community Corrections Partnership: Examining the Long-Term Effects of Youth Participation in an Afrocentric Diversion Program, *Crime and Delinquency* (2001): 558–572.

[59] Wooldredge, J., Hartman, Jennifer, Edward, L., and Holmes, S. "Effectiveness of Culturally Specific Community Treatment for African American Juvenile Felons," *Crime and Delinquency* (1994): 589–598.

[60] Nellis, A., "The Color of Justice: Racial and Ethnic Disparity in State Prisons," The Sentencing Project, 2016.

Chapter 8

[61] DeGruy, J., *Post Traumatic Slave Syndrome, Revised Edition: America's Legacy of Enduring Injury and Healing* (Joy Degruy Publications Inc., 2017).

[62] American Pychiatric Association. "Key Conceptual Frameworks and Aproaches: Cultural and Social Structural Issues," in *DSM-5-TR* (p. 16) (Washington DC: American Pychiatric Association Publishing, 2022).

[63] Sue, D. W., Arredondo, P., and McDavis, R. J., "Multicultural Counseling Competencies and Standards: A Call to the Profession," *Journal of Multicultural Counseling and Development* (1992): 64–88.

[64] Arredondo, P., Toporek, R., Brown, S. P., Jones, J., Locke, D. C., Sanchez, J., and Stadler, H., "Operationalization of the Multicultural Counseling Competencies," *Journal of Multicultural Counseling and Development* (1996): 42–78.

[65] Koslow, D. R., Salett, E. P., and International Society for Intercultural Education, T. A., "Crossing Cultures in Mental Health, SIETAR International, 1989.

[66] Ancis, J. R., "Culturally Responsive Interventions: Innovative Approaches to Working with Diverse Populations," Routledge, 2004.

[67] Shearer, R. A., and King, P. A., "Multicultural Competencies in Probation—Issues and Challenges," *Federal Probation* (2004): 3–9.

Chapter 9

[68] New York State Division of Criminal Justice Services. "Standard Specifications For Professional Probation Positions," July 6, 2024, retrieved from https://www.criminaljustice.ny.gov/opca/h10data.htm#:~:text=Probation%20Officer%20(Minority%20Group%20Specialist,probationers%20and%20communities%20upon%20assignment.

[69] Swaminathan, M., "Impact of PACE Program on Racial Disparities in the Child Welfare System," retrieved from Olmsted County, 2019, https://www.olmstedcounty.gov/sites/default/files/2021-10/PACE%20Evaluation%20Report.pdf.

[70] Mass.gov., "Specialty Courts," July 19, 2024, retrieved from https://www.mass.gov/specialty-courts.

[71] Pinal County Attorney's Office, "Specialty Courts," July 19, 2024, retrieved from https://pinalcountyattorney.org/criminal-justice/specialty-courts/.

[72] Payne, J., "Specialty Courts: Current Issues and Future Prospects," *Trends and Issues in Crime and Criminal Justice* (2006), retrieved from https://www.aic.gov.au/publications/tandi/tandi317

[73] National Center for Education Statistics, "Achievement Gaps," July 19, 2024, retrieved from https://nces.ed.gov/nationsreportcard/studies/gaps/#:~:

text=Achievement%20gaps%20occur%20when%20one,than%20the%20margin%20of%20error).

74 *Forbes*, "The Achievement Gap Hasn't Budged In 50 Years. Now What?" March 18, 2019, retrieved from https://www.forbes.com/sites/nataliewexler/2019/03/17/the-achievement-gap-hasnt-budged-in-50-years-now-what/.

75 Harlow, C. W., "Education and Correctional Populations," retrieved from Bureau of Justice Statistics, 2003, https://bjs.ojp.gov/content/pub/pdf/ecp.pdf

76 Breslow, J. M., "By the Numbers: Dropping Out of High School," retrieved from PBS, September 29, 2012, https://www.pbs.org/wgbh/frontline/article/by-the-numbers-dropping-out-of-high-school/.

77 Testoni, I., Marrella, F., Biancalan, G., Cottone, P., Alemanno, F., Mamo, D., and Grassi, L., "The Value of Dignity in Prison: A Qualitative Study with Life Convicts," *Behavioral Sciences* (2020), doi:https://doi.org/10.3390/bs10060095.

78 Angelou, M., "Still I Rise," retrieved from Poet.org, July 9, 2024, https://poets.org/poem/still-i-rise?gad_source=1&gclid=EAIaIQobChMI-IDUuP6ZhwMVWg-tBh3QKwBQEAAYASAAEgIRnfD_BwE.

79 The Three Doctors, LLC, July 19, 2024, retrieved from https://www.threedoctors.com/.

80 Bible Gateway, "Proverbs 13:12," July 9, 2024, retrieved from https://www.biblegateway.com/passage/?search=Proverbs%2013%3A12&version=NIV.

Chapter 10

81 Troccoli, K. P., "Law and Inequality: A Journal of Theory and Practice," (2002): 1–52.

82 NASW, "Standards and Indicators for Cultural Competence in Social Work Practice," National Association of Social Work, 2015.

Chapter 11

83 ISAIAH, July 19, 202), retrieved from https://isaiahmn.org/.

84 Martin Luther King Jr., "Martin Luther King Jr.'s Legacy, 20 Years On," retrieved from The Pulitzer Prizes, July 19, 2024, https://www.pulitzer.org/article/martin-luther-king-jrs-legacy-20-years.

Chapter 12

85 Phillips, J. C., *He Talk Like a White Boy* (Philadelphia, PA: Running Press, 2006).

86 Dyson, M. E., *Debating Race: with Michael Eric Dyson* (Basic Civitas Books, 2007).

Chapter 13

[87] The Three Doctors, LLC, July 19, 2024, retrieved from https://www.threedoctors.com/.

Chapter 14

[88] Angelou, M., "Still I Rise," retrieved from Poet.org, July 9, 2024, https://poets.org/poem/still-i-rise?gad_source=1&gclid=EAIaIQobChMI-IDUuP6ZhwMVWg-tBh3QKwBQEAAYASAAEgIRnfD_BwE.

ABOUT THE AUTHOR

Donavan is a licensed social worker and mitigation specialist, consultant, and trainer. For the past twenty-five years, he has worked throughout the criminal justice system and mostly with the Minnesota State Public Defender Office, Colorado Public Defender Office, and in Maricopa County Public Defender Offices. His work has included various levels of criminal defense work, including capital cases. He is also a national trainer and an adjunct faculty, teaching forensic social work, holistic defense, and criminal defense mitigation. Donavan is also trained as a DEI facilitator. His past experience includes work as a youth counselor, police officer, and juvenile residential treatment supervisor. As an extension of his career, he has made it a priority to extend his work in the community, serving on various committees and boards. He holds a master of science in educational leadership, and a doctorate in education, and is currently completing his masters in social work.

www.ingramcontent.com/pod-product-compliance
Lightning Source LLC
LaVergne TN
LVHW090354210926
848480LV00002B/336
* 9 7 9 8 8 9 5 5 3 3 1 2 3 *